GOFFSTOWN
·······R·E·B·O·R·N·······

GOFFSTOWN
········ R E B O R N ········
Transformations of a New England Town

E L I Z A B E T H   D U B R U L L E

Charleston   London

THE
History
PRESS

Published by The History Press
Charleston, SC 29403
www.historypress.net

First published 2009
Second printing 2010

Cover image: Center panel of the Heritage Quilt, created by a committee of Goffstown citizens in 1976 to honor the national bicentennial.

Manufactured in the United States

ISBN 978.1.59629.649.7

Library of Congress Cataloging-in-Publication Data

Dubrulle, Elizabeth.
Goffstown reborn : transformations of a New England town / Elizabeth Dubrulle.
p. cm.
ISBN 978-1-59629-649-7
1. Goffstown (N.H. : Town)--History. I. Title.
F44.G6D83 2009
974.2'8--dc22
2009043987

For Jackson and Vivien

Because we should all know
about the place where we grew up

CONTENTS

PREFACE

In the 1995 BBC production of Jane Austen's *Pride and Prejudice* (but not in the book), one of the characters says of her birthplace that it was "a little town, of no consequence to anyone except those fortunate enough to have lived in it." I freely admit that I had much the same expectation when I began researching this history of Goffstown. Like so many other people, I am a recent arrival to town, and my first impression of Goffstown when I saw it nearly ten years ago was that it was a charming little suburb of Manchester. After immersing myself in the town's history for the last year, though, I realize just how wrong that initial impression was. The more I read and heard about Goffstown's history, the more fascinating the story became, in no small part because Goffstown has been so many things to so many people. The complexity and variety of the town's heritage has been truly stunning.

Most New England towns have become adept at reinventing themselves, and I was prepared to find much the same story when looking at Goffstown. What I was not prepared to find was just how often and how successfully the townspeople accomplished this feat. From the first failed attempt at settlement right up through the present day, the town has participated in—and sometimes led—the trends that characterize much of New Hampshire's history. In fact, of the major agricultural, industrial, social, political, economic and cultural movements that have developed throughout New Hampshire's history, Goffstown has been involved in or at the forefront of a great number of them, as hopefully this history will show.

Thus, more than most towns in New Hampshire, Goffstown has shown its ability to continually reinvent itself. Again and again, I found that the story of Goffstown is the story of Goffstown reborn.

The fact that we know so much about Goffstown's history is due in large measure to two lifelong residents who devoted themselves to the study of this town. Goffstown's first and best-known historian was George Plummer Hadley, who wrote his two-volume history during a time when "gentlemen scholars"—usually well-educated men with the time and resources to pursue their hobbies with a great deal of enthusiasm—made numerous contributions to American history. Hadley's *History of the Town of Goffstown, 1733–1920* (published in 1922) provides a wealth of information, particularly about the town's early years. In many cases, Hadley has transcribed and reprinted early documents that might otherwise have been lost. But because he has subjected very little of this information to analysis, Hadley's work is more a primary source of historical data than a narrative history. As Dartmouth historian Jere Daniell said when he spoke in Goffstown a few years ago, Hadley's history was very useful but was also "among the strangest" local histories he had seen because it was "a rich, rich accumulation of information" in "an undigested form."

The other major contribution to the town's history comes from Douglas Earle Gove. In the second half of the twentieth century, Gove invested a tremendous amount of time interviewing the town's longtime residents and melding their recollections with his own to capture some of the historical detail so often overlooked by more traditional histories. The result was a three-volume series of books that appeared under the collective title *The Memory Bank* (published in 1998, 2000 and 2004, respectively). Gove's work is also invaluable. Too often older people, who are such important resources for local history, leave behind no record of their recollections. By taking the time to visit with them and listen to them talk about their memories, Gove has compiled an amazing record. His books are a collection of many people's stories, most of which help to illustrate Goffstown in the twentieth century. But because the book does not follow a single chronology and jumps from theme to theme, it is often difficult to get a clear picture of the town as a whole during the periods about which Gove writes.

Without these two sources, writing this book would have been a much more difficult task. With them, I have been able to weave some of their information together with the broader history of this area and with the history of the state and New England in general to create a single story of Goffstown. Not wanting to produce a huge, multivolume compendium of the town's more than 250 years, I had to limit myself to only a small collection of the many, many tales I learned about Goffstown, some of the more outrageous of which deserve mention here. I believe many people would be surprised to learn about some of the following episodes in Goffstown's history:

- In 1822, the body of a young girl, the daughter of William McDoe, was stolen from its grave at Hillside cemetery in Goffstown Center (Grasmere). It was never recovered despite the town's offer of a $500 reward.
- Sometime in the early 1900s, pranksters pulled off a tremendous feat by convincing townspeople that Gregg Pond (the future Glen Lake) had a monster in it. Although many were initially fooled, the monster turned out to be a moving contraption made out of wood and wire.
- In the 1920s, Goffstown apparently had an active chapter of the Ku Klux Klan, which was undergoing a revival all over the United States. Unlike in the South, where the Klan focused its attention on African Americans, the Klan in New Hampshire was mainly concerned with Catholics and Jews in New England society.
- A Goffstown farm saw the birth of a two-headed calf in 1925. Although the poor animal only lived for a day, it was later stuffed and became a traveling exhibit.
- In 1933, Uncanoonuc Lake temporarily disappeared. Witnesses reported seeing a churning motion in the center of the lake that lasted for several minutes, then the lake actually disappeared and reappeared. The most commonly accepted explanation for this odd occurrence was that the water momentary drained into an underground cavern and then was somehow forced back up to the earth's surface.
- On November 1, 1973, two Goffstown residents claim to have had contact with aliens. One woman said she saw a faceless man standing on her porch, while another woman reported seeing a spaceship hover over her car on Mast Road and then shoot off into the night.

One day, I hope these stories may receive fuller treatment than they have to date, along with all the other wonderful tales of Goffstown, even those that don't fall in the "weird and wacky" category. These items did not appear in the body of this book because they did not fit into the narrative structure I was trying to impose, but they were simply too fantastic to leave out altogether. Many of them are so unsubstantiated as to be nothing more than local legends, but all of them would serve as interesting topics of research.

The narrative I present here can serve as a framework for all of these stories and others, providing context and background to gain a better understanding of Goffstown's larger story. In other words, this book is not intended to be the last word in Goffstown's history; it's intended to be the first, a starting point for those wanting to become better acquainted with the town's heritage.

As with almost any project, I could not have completed this book on my own. Many people assisted me along the way and did so with a graciousness and patience that does them credit.

Several people at The History Press helped this book get published. Lance Warren originally conceived the idea for the project and approached me about doing it. Without his encouragement, I probably would never have dreamed of taking on such an endeavor. His successor, Brianna Cullen, helped usher the project through to completion, answering my many queries with promptness and good humor. Ryan Finn did a wonderful job copyediting the manuscript and helping me smooth over the rough patches. Marshall Hudson created the beautiful maps for the book.

Eleanor Porritt and Barbara Mace from the Goffstown Historical Society generously allowed me to reprint many of the photographs that appear in these pages. They also answered my questions, helped set me straight a few times and gave me the benefit of both their accumulated knowledge of Goffstown and the incredible archive they have compiled.

The wonderful staff at the Goffstown Public Library, particularly Dianne Hathaway (who suggested me to Lance Warren for this project) and Sandy Whipple, were thoroughly helpful and pleasant, no matter how many books I ordered or questions I asked.

The outstanding staff at the Saint Anselm College Library—including, but not limited to, Keith Chevalier, Martha Dickerson and the indefatigable Sue Gagnon—have mastered the art of combining professionalism and friendliness. Their assistance in gathering research material for this book was indispensable.

Several people also took the time to speak with me about Goffstown history or their areas of expertise, including Professor Meoghan Cronin (English Department at Saint Anselm College and an active member of the

Villa Augustina community), Professor Joe Spoerl (Philosophy Department at Saint Anselm College), Professor Beth Salerno (History Department at Saint Anselm College), Stephen Taylor (New Hampshire's resident authority on the great sheep boom), Dan LaRochelle (Pinardville historian and owner of King Lanes Bowling, located right next to the site of Edmond Pinard's original store), Kristen McLane (former president of the Villa Augustina Home and School group), Peter A. Wallner (Franklin Pierce scholar and librarian at the New Hampshire Historical Society) and Robbie Grady (director of the Goffstown Main Street Program).

For others, their contributions lay mainly in the realm of good cheer, encouragement and hand-holding. Meg Cronin and Roseann Latona fulfilled their usual roles in my life by lending a sympathetic ear for all my problems, making me laugh even when I didn't want to and plying me with large amounts of red wine. My colleagues on the Goffstown Historic District Commission could be a whole cheerleading squad unto themselves. While at the playground or the beach, my steadfast friends in Sanity Savers listened patiently to all of my historical musings about how interesting Goffstown was. One Sanity Saver in particular, Brittany Casey, read the manuscript thoroughly and provided several suggested revisions. So too did my colleague at the Colonial Society of Massachusetts, Editor of Publications John W. Tyler, who read the first half of the manuscript and, with his knowledge of New England history, saved me from making several errors.

And finally, many family members gave me encouragement while I worked on this project and offered their assistance. In particular, my parents, Jim and Norma Marshall, cheered me on, watched my children so I could write and helped me track down information (it helps to have a mother who is a librarian and a father who studies trains and transportation systems). But most importantly, my husband listened to me talk about this project for many, many months; read drafts and discussed ideas with me; took breaks from his own work to watch the kids and give me time to write; and gave me all the benefits of both his exquisite mind and his loving care.

Naturally, any errors contained within these pages are entirely my own.

SHOVETOWN:
THE TOWN THAT WASN'T

E dward Shove was a happy man. For six long years, he had pestered, wheedled, cajoled, bullied, pushed and begged his colleagues in the Massachusetts General Court to award grants of land from the disputed territory of New Hampshire to veterans of King Philip's War. The war had been over for more than fifty years, and most of those veterans were long dead, but their heirs were still very much alive and could profit from a new land venture, Edward Shove among them. The land grants could also bolster Massachusetts's claims to the territory, especially if the land was settled by good Massachusetts farmers. So on this spring day of April 26, 1733, Edward Shove breathed a sigh of satisfaction as the Massachusetts General Court authorized grants for the establishment of seven towns, the so-called Narragansett Grants.

There was no question, at least in the American colonists' minds, that the land was theirs for the taking. In 1497, an Italian explorer who has been remembered through history by his anglicized name of Sebastian Cabot sailed to the New World and claimed what would become New England for the British Crown. It would be more than 120 years until the first Englishmen actually settled there, but eventually the Pilgrims did come in 1620 and amidst much hardship founded the first permanent English settlement in New England. Ten years later, a much larger, more prosperous wave of Puritan immigrants landed in what would become Boston and quickly spread settlements across the region.

While all this was going on in Massachusetts, New Hampshire was being settled slowly and more modestly. In 1606, the British Crown awarded a massive land grant to two entrepreneurs named Ferdinando Gorges and John Mason that encompassed a huge portion of northern New England, although its specifics were unclear because no one really knew much about the geography of the New England interior at the time. Sailors had brought back fairly accurate accounts of the coastline and the first few miles inland, but farther west than that was a complete mystery. So the western boundary of the Gorges-Mason grant was a little vague, with some people viewing the grant as extending west all the way to what would become New York while others contended that it only went about sixty miles inland.

In 1629, Gorges and Mason split their grant, with Gorges taking everything north of the Piscataqua River (present-day Maine) and Mason taking everything south of it to the Massachusetts border, which was designated as three miles north of the Merrimack River. Unfortunately, the grant didn't specify which part of the Merrimack River, and no one knew at the time that the Merrimack River ran north to south, not east to west. Hence, the troubling problem of geography led to a land dispute that was to come and go for about the next one hundred years.

At one point in the latter part of the seventeenth century, New Hampshire even became part of Massachusetts as Norfolk County, although most of the time New Hampshire existed as a separate province, with four struggling settlements all located near the seacoast. But there was still that troubling question of where the boundary between the two colonies should be. As the colonists explored deeper inland, they made the puzzling discovery of the Merrimack's true course, which threw the whole issue of land rights into confusion. Massachusetts insisted that its northern boundary was three miles north of the *source* of the Merrimack (Lake Winnipesaukee), while New Hampshire was equally insistent that its southern boundary was three miles north of the *mouth* of the Merrimack (present-day Newburyport). The difference between these two views comprises about half of what is today southern New Hampshire.

By the 1720s, a few settlers had started to push into this region, and both governments had started to worry that their claims would not be respected. Massachusetts was by far the better established and wealthier colony, and it launched a two-pronged effort to secure the territory for

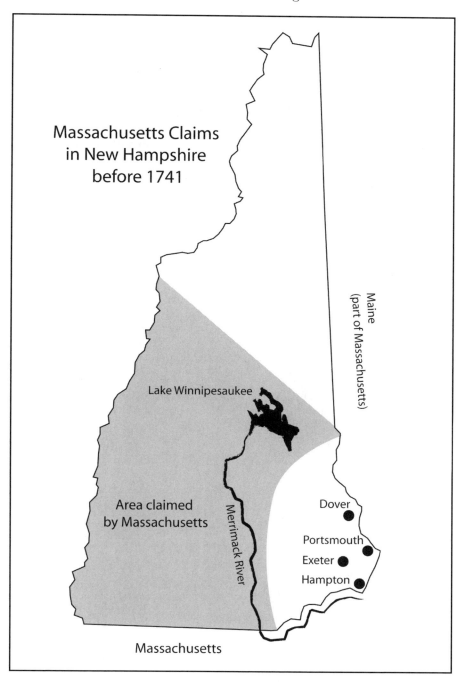

Massachusetts claimed an enormous amount of territory in the first part of the eighteenth century that was eventually awarded to New Hampshire. *Map created by Marshall Hudson.*

itself. First, it ordered its agents in England to use their influence with government officials to bring about a favorable outcome; such lobbying was not at all uncommon at the time. Second, it started issuing grants of land in the region to get Massachusetts settlers established there.

As luck would have it, the Massachusetts government had long before promised land grants to the veterans of King Philip's War, the last big Indian conflict in southern New England, which had occurred during 1675–76. Even though fifty years had passed without a single grant being awarded, the 1720s seemed a propitious time to finally make good on that promise. Because much of the war took place in the Narragansett region of Rhode Island, the conflict was also known as the Narragansett War. By the time it was over, most of the Indians in southern New England had either been killed or sold into slavery and their tribal organizations disbanded. The war also took a heavy toll on the colonists, with nearly half of all the towns in Massachusetts suffering from an Indian attack at some point during the conflict. At the height of the war, in an effort to encourage colonists to join the militia and fight the Indians, the Massachusetts government had promised a grant of land to each soldier. In 1685, nearly ten years after the war had ended, legislators made a half-hearted attempt to make good on that promise, but the effort petered out. Then, in 1725, the idea of issuing grants to these soldiers arose again, with the added bonus of placing Massachusetts settlers within the territory disputed by New Hampshire.

Edward Shove from Dighton, Massachusetts, an influential figure in the House of Representatives in the 1720s, was in the forefront of this effort. Having been born in 1680, he had not been involved in King Philip's War himself; his connection to the soldiers seems to have come through his wife's father, Theophilus Mitchell. Nevertheless, he doggedly pursued the claims to land over the next several years, serving on nearly every committee the House formed to further the matter. When the House first addressed the issue in earnest in 1727 and 1728, there were thought to be just 240 soldiers or their heirs who could make claims to land. The House accordingly decided that two townships should be created for these people, 120 claimants in each. But as word got out that the General Court was actually going to give out the land it had promised so long ago, more claimants and their heirs came forward, and by 1732 the number had swelled to 840 claimants. In response, the House enlarged the number of townships to seven, a decision reached on April 26, 1733.

The seven townships were called the Narragansett Grants. Until such time as the settlers could decide on names for their new towns, they were referred to simply as Narragansett No. 1, Narragansett No. 2 and so on. A month and a half later, on June 6, the 840 claimants met on Boston Common, organized themselves into groups of 120, elected three men from each group to act as their representatives and pulled lots out of a hat for the seven townships. Shove, serving as one of the representatives for his group, acquired Narragansett No. 4, which was immediately dubbed Shovetown in his honor.

No one really knew just what their new township looked like, though. The area had not been surveyed, and given such imperfect knowledge of geography in the wilds of northern New England, the economic value of Narragansett No. 4 was anybody's guess. Very few of the proprietors intended to live in the new township themselves. For most of them, interest in this land was purely speculative. They hoped to encourage the establishment of a modest settlement and then sell their land at a profit. Much of New England, after that first wave of settlement in the seventeenth century, had been colonized in the same way. The American tendency to produce many children, all of whom would need land of their own someday, meant that there was a continual market of prospective settlers always looking for a promising place in which to settle and farm.

First, though, the claimants needed to see what they had to offer prospective settlers. In 1734, Shove organized a small group to survey Narragansett No. 4. Whether he accompanied them or not is unknown, but the results of the survey were not promising. On December 16, 1735, Shove, acting on behalf of his fellow claimants, petitioned the Massachusetts General Court for a new parcel of land, claiming that Narragansett No. 4 had proven "so poor and barren, as to be altogether uncapable [*sic*] of making settlements." Two years later, the House complied, rescinding the grant to Narragansett No. 4 and awarding the claimants a new tract of land, this time in Massachusetts (the majority of which today lies beneath the waters of the Quabbin Reservoir).

So just what did the surveyors see that convinced them to give back the land they had been granted? The township was approximately six square miles, or roughly twenty-nine thousand acres. Like most of New Hampshire, the ground was rocky and the soil barely passable for productive farming. There were dense forests, though, of good solid New England pine, chestnut, oak, maple and birch. The twin peaks of the Uncanoonuc Mountains rose high above any other elevation in the region. The township was bisected by the Piscataquog River (the Indian word for "great deer place"), providing fresh water, fish and potential power for sawmills and gristmills. The township's eastern border extended all the way to the far side of the Merrimack River and included nearly five miles along the banks of the river itself. By far the greatest natural resource of the township was Amoskeag Falls on the Merrimack. The falls, said to be the most powerful waterfall in New England, were full of fish, particularly salmon and shad, and had long been one of the principal meeting grounds and ceremonial sites for the region's Native Americans.

By the 1730s, there weren't many Indians left in the region, although it had once been home to several thousand. The township's land had been populated by the Namoskeags, a seminomadic tribe who hunted, fished, camped and engaged in limited agriculture in the area, moving between different locations with the seasons. They had a large camp on the wide plain north of the Piscataquog River shortly before it divides into two branches, another camp on Harry Brook where it empties into the Piscataquog and a third camp on the banks of the Merrimack River near Amoskeag Falls (all three sites would later become village centers in Goffstown). The Namoskeags were part of the larger Penacook Confederacy that encompassed all the tribes in the Merrimack Valley. The Penacooks' main camp was located near present-day Concord, and at the time Europeans arrived to settle New England in the early seventeenth century, there may have been as many as twelve thousand people in the Penacook Confederacy. Every spring, all of the various tribes within the confederacy gathered at Amoskeag Falls to fish and pay allegiance to their chief, who for most of the seventeenth century was Passaconaway, the famed Penacook leader of northern New England. Legend holds that one spring when the tribes had gathered at Amoskeag (probably about 1685) a young Indian woman named Rimmon threw herself off the large rock formation located on the west side of the river. She had been thwarted in love by Passaconaway's son, Wonalancet, who married her elder sister Mineola instead. Ever after, the rock from which she plunged to her death has been called Rock Rimmon in her honor.

The seventeenth century was not kind to the Indians. European settlers unknowingly brought disease, most notably smallpox, that literally wiped out entire native villages in a matter of months, including most of the Namoskeags. Such catastrophes led to political reorganization, particularly since the arrival of Europeans altered the balance of power between tribal groups and forced Native Americans to leave their traditional areas. Plague following displacement quickly led to warfare, and the Penacooks spent several decades in the middle of the seventeenth century trying to fend off a Mohawk offensive. By 1685, they had suffered such devastating losses to disease and warfare that many of those remaining went north to join the remnants of other Indian tribes who were creating a new settlement known as St. Francis in Quebec. Some Native Americans were still present in the Merrimack Valley in the 1730s and 1740s, but they were generally hunting and fishing parties that had wandered down from their new northern home.

There were almost no white settlers in this region of the Merrimack Valley at the time Shove ordered his survey of Narragansett No. 4. A few individual land grants had been extended to men hoping to settle near Amoskeag Falls, since they no doubt recognized the tremendous potential of this great natural force, but they had not actually built anything by this point. Likewise, a few others had petitioned for grants near the mouth of the Piscataquog where it met the Merrimack, but again they had not yet settled there. The most significant land grant was awarded to the town of Medford, Massachusetts, in June 1735, since the town hoped to settle some of its younger sons there. Although the town was awarded a one-thousand-acre spread that was named Medford Farms, Medford later sold the land to other settlers without having moved any of its own people.

So why did Shove and his fellow proprietors decide that the land was unsuitable for further development? Perhaps we'll never know, but by December 1737, Narragansett No. 4 was a township in limbo without anyone promoting its settlement.

JOHN GOFFE AND THE FOUNDING OF GOFFSTOWN

Narragansett No. 4's fate was not all that uncommon. The Massachusetts General Court had been issuing land grants all over southern New Hampshire in the 1730s. Bedford and Amherst had also been Narragansett townships. Additionally, there was a series of frontier townships located farther west: Warner, Bradford, Acworth, Alstead, Hopkinton, Henniker, Hillsborough, Washington and Lempster—all were granted by Massachusetts in 1736, this time to veterans of King William's War against the French in the 1690s. Not only did the frontier townships serve to bolster Massachusetts's claims to the land, but they were also intended as buffer settlements between the Merrimack Valley and the Indians farther west and north. Very few of these townships can actually date their settlement back to these grants, though. Most suffered more or less the same fate as Narragansett No. 4: few people actually moved there and started the arduous work of carving out homesteads.

In the end, Massachusetts's efforts were all for naught. In 1737, the British Crown severed all relation between the governments of Massachusetts and New Hampshire. The two had had separate legislatures but a single governor for years, but even this tie was cut after 1737 when the Crown appointed a new governor for New Hampshire. Yet Massachusetts still hoped that the boundary controversy would be settled in its favor, thus securing all the fertile land and resources of the Merrimack Valley for itself.

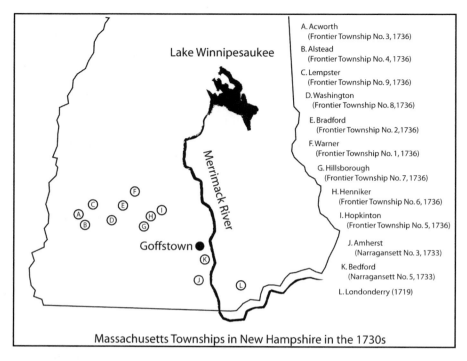

A. Acworth
(Frontier Township No. 3, 1736)

B. Alstead
(Frontier Township No. 4, 1736)

C. Lempster
(Frontier Township No. 9, 1736)

D. Washington
(Frontier Township No. 8, 1736)

E. Bradford
(Frontier Township No. 2, 1736)

F. Warner
(Frontier Township No. 1, 1736)

G. Hillsborough
(Frontier Township No. 7, 1736)

H. Henniker
(Frontier Township No. 6, 1736)

I. Hopkinton
(Frontier Township No. 5, 1736)

J. Amherst
(Narragansett No. 3, 1733)

K. Bedford
(Narragansett No. 5, 1733)

L. Londonderry (1719)

Lake Winnipesaukee

Merrimack River

Goffstown

Massachusetts Townships in New Hampshire in the 1730s

Many of the towns in southern New Hampshire can date their foundings from the Massachusetts grants of the 1730s, even though few were actually settled as a result. *Map created by Marshall Hudson.*

It was not to be, however. In 1741, the Crown rejected Massachusetts's claims and awarded the whole region to New Hampshire, with the border between the two colonies established near the mouth of the Merrimack River rather than at its source.

In the midst of all this uncertainty, settlers still came to the Merrimack Valley, lured by the promise of land and resources. One of the first was an adventurous young man named John Goffe. After several years' residence in Londonderry, where his family had been among the initial settlers when the town was founded in 1719, Goffe had begun exploring the area north of Londonderry. He eventually decided to settle his growing family there near Cohass Brook (at a spot now known as Goff's Falls) in 1734. He also made a claim for a large portion of land in what would become the town of Derryfield. Although his new homestead flourished, Goffe jumped at the chance to buy land in Bedford, just across the river. By 1738, just one year after the Walker brothers established the first permanent settlement in Bedford, Goffe had become one of the largest landowners in the community.

Transformations of a New England Town

John Goffe was a man of many talents, not the least of which was his ability to recognize a profitable venture when he saw one. In his long life, he was involved in the establishment of nearly a dozen new towns in New Hampshire, buying numerous parcels of land all over the province (he held over one hundred deeds in 1771); serving as a justice of the peace, town moderator and selectman; convening—and sometimes hosting at his own home—town meetings; sponsoring and partnering others in such vital industries as sawmills, gristmills, forges and a ferry service; and bringing itinerant preachers to communities. He was also an avid backwoodsman, earning for himself the sobriquet "Hunter John Goffe." A formidable military commander, he mentored such well-known frontier heroes as Robert Rogers and John Stark. In sum, he was arguably the most revered and respected man in the Merrimack Valley during this period.

In the late 1740s, Goffe turned his focus on the still unpopulated and ungranted land of Narragansett No. 4. He knew the area well, having hunted there extensively, and he saw no reason why it could not be settled as Derryfield and Bedford had been, even though no one had seemed much interested in it since Shove and his compatriots repudiated it in 1737.

With Massachusetts out of the picture by 1741, the only claim on the land was made by John Tufton Mason, a descendant of the John Mason who had held the first claims to New Hampshire back in the 1620s. John Tufton Mason reasserted his rights to the land that had been claimed by Massachusetts, but this time no one contested him. In 1746, he sold the entire grant to a group of twelve Portsmouth merchants who thereafter became known as the Masonian Proprietors. These men included among their ranks some of the most influential and wealthiest figures in the province, including Governor Benning Wentworth. They hoped to increase the population and prestige of New Hampshire by encouraging settlement throughout the colony, and they saw no reason why they shouldn't grow rich doing it. Over the next few years, the Masonian Proprietors gave away huge portions of the original grant, reserving for themselves prime lots within each settlement that they planned to sell off later when the settlements became well established and the value of the land had risen.

On December 3, 1748, the Masonian Proprietors gave the township of Narragansett No. 4 to a collection of forty-six town proprietors, a group of investors from a total of nine towns in New Hampshire and Massachusetts. By far the largest contingent hailed from Bedford, and this collection of fourteen would also be the most active in the town's development in its early years. All of the Bedford grantees were friends or relatives of John

Goffe, and he seemed to have been the driving force behind securing the grant. The first name listed on the grant, however, was that of the Reverend Thomas Parker from Dracut, Massachusetts, who probably received this honor because of his position as a minister, even though he apparently had little to do with attaining the grant or initiating the town's settlement. Nevertheless, few could dispute Goffe's leading role in the endeavor. In a series of meetings in the winter of 1748–49, held mostly in Portsmouth (the province's capital) but sometimes in Bedford, Goffe served as moderator in nearly every one while the town proprietors organized the settlement of the community. Thus, fifteen years after it was originally granted, Narragansett No. 4 became a town, and Goffstown had been reborn.

The town proprietors recognized the Medford grant of 1735 and a few other land grants that had been made before 1748, but otherwise they could begin their settlement from scratch, with no remnants of the original grant. The terms of the current grant—the Masonian grant—were very specific and mirrored those of nearly every other township granted by the Masonian Proprietors. The first order of business was to survey the township and divide it into sixty-eight lots, each lot composed of three shares of 100 to 150 acres each. The acreage varied due to the presence of such natural features as lakes, rivers, swamps, mountains and so on; lots that contained such unusable—and unfarmable—features were made larger to compensate. Nineteen shares were reserved for the Masonian Proprietors, two shares were set aside for the minister's personal use and the church's support, one share was designated for the benefit of the town's school and the remaining forty-six shares were to be divided among the town proprietors. Accordingly, at a proprietors' meeting held in Portsmouth on July 13, 1749, the forty-six men drew for their lots. To ensure that no one ended up with a bad parcel of land, though, they drew for lots rather than shares, meaning that each man drew three times, and consequently his share would be divided into three separate lots scattered throughout the town.

The other conditions of the grant included requirements that each town proprietor clear a specified amount of land for farming within one-, two- and four-year increments and that he build a home of substantial dimensions (which were specifically laid out in the grant) within one year. Collectively, the town proprietors were required to put up thirty pounds each to cover the costs of a survey, building a meetinghouse, laying out roads and constructing bridges. In addition, the proprietors were required to build a meetinghouse within two years and specify where such community features as a school, burying ground and training field would be established.

Transformations of a New England Town

With many of the details finalized by mid-1749, the town proprietors could get to work establishing the new town. A few people were already living there. Local tradition holds that one man moved somewhere into the interior of Narragansett No. 4 in 1741, although who he was, where he lived and what happened to him remains a mystery. Joseph Kennedy from Bedford started clearing land for a farm just north of the Bedford line sometime in the early 1740s, but he didn't actually start living on the property until sometime later. Instead, he returned to the garrison house in Bedford every night, fearing an Indian attack. Such raids remained a major concern for colonists during this period, even though Native Americans no longer resided in the region. The French, holding all of what is today Canada and the Ohio and Mississippi Valleys, had done a better job of cultivating Indian allies throughout the colonial period than had the British. So when Britain and France were at war, which was quite frequently during the seventeenth and eighteenth centuries, France's Indian allies joined in the fight against the British and their colonists. Northern New England periodically saw Native American war parties sweep south from St. Francis, either killing American settlers or taking them to Canada as captives, usually for ransom. In the 1740s, raiding parties were still venturing as far south as Pembroke and Hopkinton, which was close enough to strike terror into the settlers in Goffstown, Bedford and Derryfield.

To guard themselves from Indian attack, the colonists built garrison houses, which were nothing more than high stockade fences placed around the most substantial house in the region. These houses had been provisioned with food and supplies and cleared of surrounding trees and brush to deny the enemy cover in an attack. Any report of Indian sightings in a region would send the settlers fleeing to the garrison house with their families. In Bedford, the garrison house was owned by John Goffe, yet another indication of his status in the region.

Even before the Masonian Proprietors had granted Narragansett No. 4, the community was becoming known as Goffe's pet project. In a letter dated November 29, 1748, one of Goffe's fellow investors, Joseph Blanchard, referred to the area as "Goffe's town." The name apparently stuck. For the next fifteen years, the community was called Goffe's Town, sometimes with the final "e" on Goffe's name and sometimes without, until it began to consistently appear in the town records as the single word "Goffstown" in 1764.

These years proved incredibly busy for the town proprietors who lived nearby and could thus take an active role in establishing the community.

James Karr was one of the few town proprietors who actually moved to Goffstown, building this house in 1748, even before the proprietors had received their grant from the Masonian Proprietors. The large barn, originally located across the road from the main house, often served as a gathering place before the meetinghouse was built in 1769.

Only fifteen of the proprietors, or roughly one-third, moved to Goffstown themselves. The rest either sold their land or settled family members on it. Those who lived on the land undertook the arduous tasks of removing trees and rocks to clear fields for planting and building houses and barns. It was grueling, backbreaking work that often resulted in just enough farmable land to survive. But even for those who were not carving homesteads out of the wilderness, there was plenty to do, and some of the men from Bedford, such as the town clerk Matthew Patten, were very active indeed.

Within the first ten years of the settlement, the proprietors tried to establish a sawmill on the Piscataquog River, which was essential with all the building going on. They laid out the first two roads, running along the north and south sides of the Piscataquog, by 1752, and a few others connecting Goffstown to the surrounding towns soon after. They also tried to establish the basic services that people would expect in the mid-eighteenth century such as church services, a burying ground, a school, a meetinghouse, bridges, a gristmill and a forge; most importantly, they promoted the town so that new settlers would come and buy their land. The culmination of these activities was a slow but steady growth for Goffstown in the 1750s, despite the fact that the French and Indian War had erupted in northern New England, drawing off many of the region's men to go and fight.

Not surprisingly, the local commander was John Goffe, who began the war as a captain in command of a company and ended it as a full colonel in command of a regiment. Goffe recruited heavily from Derryfield, Bedford and Goffstown, and many of the men were his friends or family. He led them through nearly all of the major engagements of the war that occurred in New England, from the Battle of Lake George in 1755 to the massacre at Fort William Henry in 1757 to the building of the Crown Point Road in 1760. Of Goffstown's fledgling population in the 1750s, eleven men served at some point during the French and Indian War under Goffe, which was a significant proportion. By the time the war was over, Goffe had gained more renown than ever, and Goffstown was ready to come into its own.

DUELING CONGREGATIONS

Although the French and Indian War didn't officially end until 1763, the fighting in New England, New York and Canada was over by 1760. The end of the war brought a new level of security to the people of New Hampshire. The French had been defeated and lost their North American possessions, so New Englanders no longer worried about the enemy on their northern border. France's Indian allies had been all but destroyed by the conflict, especially the few who lived adjacent to New England. Without the support of the French government, the remnants of these eastern tribes lived peaceably in small reservations far from English settlements.

Such peace brought more people to New Hampshire, as all the land between the Atlantic Ocean and the Hudson River was now secure for settlement. Goffstown was one of those communities to benefit from the influx. Even through the 1750s, the little town had made slow but steady progress. By 1760, the town proprietors were seriously outnumbered by the newcomers who bought their land from them and made their investment in the town profitable. Not surprisingly, the new residents started clamoring for more say in Goffstown's decisions and moved to incorporate the community as a town. They applied for a charter from the king through Governor Benning Wentworth in Portsmouth. The British Crown granted the charter on June 16, 1761, turning over the running of the town to its residents and ending the administration of the town proprietors. This was not a revolution but a natural progression. Many towns in New England were chartered in much the same way, and it was expected that once the residents of a community had established it on a firm footing they would apply for a charter and begin governing themselves. In fact, it was exactly what the town proprietors hoped would happen, because the value of their land, which was the point of this whole exercise of creating a township, would be higher in a stable, established community than in a frontier settlement. Although many of the proprietors continued to own land in Goffstown, and the ones from surrounding towns like Bedford still offered assistance to the town when called upon, almost all of these men stepped back from the management of the town's affairs after incorporation, including Goffe, who had always been an active leader in the town despite being gone from the area for at least six months a year while on campaign during the war.

At the time of its incorporation, Goffstown was home to about two hundred people living on roughly thirty to forty farms. They had settled all over town, but three fledgling villages, which were actually more like crossroads with perhaps an inn, were starting to emerge: one along the banks of the Merrimack River known as Amoskeag; one at the other end of town called the West Village near the line with New Boston and Weare at a spot where a ford allowed for relatively easy passage over the Piscataquog River; and the main settlement of the town right in the middle of the township, where Harry Brook met the Piscataquog in an area today known as Grasmere but then referred to as Goffstown Center. Some of the new residents had moved to Goffstown from surrounding communities, others had come up from settlements in Massachusetts and still others had arrived from the Scotch-Irish community in Londonderry.

Did the town have a distinctive character in these early years of its existence? Hardly. Most of its residents barely even recognized the idea of township at this point. Many of the people who came to Goffstown had connections with others in the Merrimack Valley, particularly with residents of Derryfield or Bedford, and it was with these friends and family that they felt a sense of community. Town boundaries seemed less important than settling a homestead on good land, and town affairs only occasionally disturbed the hard work of carving out an existence on a new farm. But with the townspeople running things for themselves, a major divide quickly became apparent among the residents, one that would color almost every aspect of town affairs for the next several decades.

The settlers from Massachusetts saw themselves as being of good English stock. Many of their ancestors had arrived in the New World in one of the waves of Puritan immigration that populated Massachusetts in the seventeenth century. They were almost all Congregationalists, as were most of the settlers who came to New Hampshire in the eighteenth century, and they held a slight majority in the town.

The settlers from Londonderry, however, had an entirely different background, being of Scotch-Irish origin. Their ancestors were originally Presbyterians from Scotland who had moved to northern Ireland in the early seventeenth century, encouraged by the British government to populate Ireland with reliable British subjects to keep the Irish in check. The Scotch-Irish, therefore, were neither Irish nor Catholic, but the English still viewed them with some ambivalence. Scots were stereotypically portrayed as a rough, violent, slightly backward people, well suited for a hard life on the frontier but not so well suited to the more civilized existence of a settled town. This view was even more pronounced where the Scotch-Irish were concerned, since they had had to deal with the semibarbaric (and Catholic) Irish for so long. The English settlers from Massachusetts saw the Scotch-Irish as different from themselves—different in temperament, different in character, different in religion—and these differences had very little to do with theology and a great deal to do with culture. In short, the English viewed the Scots as holding beliefs and values that were not entirely compatible with those of Puritan New Englanders.

In 1718, the first Scotch-Irish emigrants arrived in New England. By the following year, they had purchased land for a settlement of their own in what was referred to as chestnut country in New Hampshire. They initially called their new settlement Nutfield when they arrived there in 1719, but when the town was incorporated in 1721, they adopted a name from the old country: Londonderry. Over the next several decades, thousands of Scotch-Irish came to America, and many of them went through Londonderry on their way to finding more permanent homes. From this base, Londonderry supplied a steady stream of new settlers for the rest of the Merrimack Valley, settlers who bore their Scotch-Irish ancestry proudly and resented the condescension of the English Puritans.

In almost every community in the region, this split between the Massachusetts Congregationalists and the Scotch-Irish Presbyterians proved a source of contention. Derryfield, in fact, was so crippled by the divisiveness that its development was noticeably slowed. New settlers opted to find other communities to put down roots rather than join one that was riven by arguments and disputes. In Goffstown, the division between the two communities was very apparent even in the pattern of settlement: the Massachusetts Congregationalists bought land on the north side of the Piscataquog, while the Scotch-Irish Presbyterians settled on the south side.

Such distinct groupings were sure to lead to conflict and did, first over the location of the meetinghouse.

Contrary to the terms of the initial grant of 1748 from the Masonian Proprietors, the community had not managed to build a meetinghouse within the specified time period of two years. Such a delay was not at all uncommon. Although nearly every community had a similar requirement in its grant, very few of them actually met it. As long as settlement continued in the town and there was an increasing demand for land, the Masonian Proprietors didn't care much about enforcing the other provisions of the grant.

Goffstown, however, took longer than most communities to build a meetinghouse, in part because of the division between Congregationalists and Presbyterians. By 1766, the issue had become a major source of contention in the community. Both sides agreed that the meetinghouse should be located somewhere near Goffstown Center, but the big question was whether it should be on the north side or the south side of the river. More was at stake than mere geography; the location of the meetinghouse corresponded in some degree to the matter of influence. A subtle war was being waged for the heart and soul of the town. Would it be predominantly a Congregational (i.e., English) community? Or would it be a Presbyterian (i.e., Scotch-Irish) community? The determination of the meetinghouse's location would more or less settle that question, because once the meetinghouse had been built, it would become the focal point for the community. It would be there where town meetings and any business of importance would be transacted. It would be there where the town center would emerge with the establishment of the town common, the burying ground, possibly the school and most likely any taverns or other businesses. But most important, the meetinghouse served as the community's church until a town was prosperous enough to build a separate structure, which could be several decades away. So if the church was located on the north side of the river, it would most likely hire a Congregational minister because more Congregationalists would be likely to attend, given its relative proximity to their homes. The same held true for Presbyterians on the south side of the river.

For the next two years, the issue of which side of the river would hold the meetinghouse dominated town politics. The matter was finally settled when James Karr, a prosperous farmer who hosted many town meetings and prayer sessions in his spacious barn, donated a parcel of land to the town for the building's construction. It was located on the north side of the river. Even the Presbyterians couldn't argue with a free gift of land, and

A nineteenth-century photograph of Goffstown's first meetinghouse.

construction began in 1768. Although it wasn't completely finished until 1772, the townspeople began using the building in early August 1769. A large plain structure approximately thirty feet by ten feet, the meetinghouse had a gallery, pews and a pulpit but no heat.

Once the meetinghouse had been built, the townspeople turned their attention to the next problem: choosing a minister. In the years before the meetinghouse was constructed, residents had made do with only occasional religious services, usually held in someone's barn or house and led by one of the many roaming, or itinerant, preachers traveling throughout the area. Now with a dedicated place of worship, the impetus for a settled minister became stronger. A 1714 New Hampshire law dictated that every taxpaying resident of a town must help support a minister financially, and each town's minister should be chosen by majority vote. Congregationalists were in the majority in Goffstown, but because of the large Presbyterian minority, an effort was made to find a minister who would be acceptable to both denominations. Unfortunately, a consensus proved elusive. After months of bickering between the two factions, the Congregationalists offered the position to a young minister from Amesbury, Massachusetts, named Joseph Currier, who had recently graduated from Harvard. The Presbyterians found this choice unacceptable and petitioned the General Court in November 1771 to relieve them of the tax to support the town's minister. Instead, they hoped to build their own church and hire their own minister, thus establishing two town-supported ministries. The

Congregationalists argued that Goffstown could ill afford such an expense, and the General Court agreed. The petition was denied, and yet strangely, residents at the town meeting in March voted to exempt the Presbyterians from the tax the following year, which is just what the Presbyterians had sought in the first place.

Even with this relief, the Presbyterians never did manage to build their own church in town, and they relied on itinerant preachers or traveled to nearby Bedford, which was a solidly Presbyterian town, for services. The small groups of Anabaptists and Methodists in Goffstown also relied on itinerant preachers, neither group being large enough to support its own minister. Ironically, even the Congregationalists came to the conclusion that Currier had not been a good choice after all. He had been hired on a three-year contract, but he turned out to be "intemperate" and his contract was not renewed when it expired in 1774. It's unclear whether "intemperate" meant he drank too much or spoke too carelessly. Either characteristic could prove inconvenient in a minister, especially if he were the only one in town.

Even with Currier gone and the Congregationalists opting to rely on itinerant preachers instead of a settled minister, relations between the two groups remained tense, although they did reach an agreement to divide the use of the meetinghouse between them, with the Congregationalists using it for their preaching two-thirds of the time and the Presbyterians using it the other third. The Anabaptists and the Methodists were only allowed to use it if no one else was, which gives a good indication of the groups' relative status in town.

GOFFSTOWN FIGHTS THE
AMERICAN REVOLUTION

The religious differences that divided the community did not undermine the town's unity on another issue that became more and more prominent in the early 1770s: Britain's relationship to its American colonies.

Like many of the American colonists, New Hampshire residents had grown increasingly dissatisfied with British rule in the 1760s and early 1770s. With the French no longer a threat on the North American continent after their defeat in the French and Indian War in 1763, British attempts to raise taxes and impose tighter controls on colonial trade seemed an unforgivable interference for many Americans. The residents of the Merrimack Valley had an additional grievance that was keenly felt in Goffstown: the British control of timber for ships' masts.

Between 1699 and 1729, the British Crown had enacted a series of laws curtailing colonists' rights to the timber on their land. By the middle of the eighteenth century, when Goffstown was being developed, the laws mandated that no one except specially licensed royal mast agents could cut down white pine trees wider than twenty-four inches in diameter, measuring twelve inches off the ground. Furthermore, before cutting any trees on a property, the owner was required to hire a royal surveyor to inspect the property and mark each of these large trees with three notches in a pattern known as the broad arrow—hence the name of the policy regarding large white pine trees became known as the king's broad arrow policy. If a property owner was caught ignoring the law and began cutting trees without paying for the survey, he would forfeit his entire lot. The enforcement of these laws was the responsibility of the surveyor general of the king's woods, a lucrative position held by New Hampshire's own governor through this time period. The surveyor general employed deputy surveyors who traveled around the province conducting surveys and checking the sawmills to make sure no protected logs were illegally used by the colonists. For those caught with protected trees at the sawmill, a fine almost always followed and the trees were turned over to the Crown. The reservation of the masts for the king's use was reiterated in the town's 1761 charter, in case anyone hoped to ignore the earlier laws governing the trade.

The British government rigorously enforced this policy because of the need for ships' masts for its fast-growing navy in the eighteenth century. Each ship of the line, which comprised Britain's mighty naval fleet, required a new mast every fifteen to twenty years, even if a storm or enemy action hadn't already mandated its replacement. Harvesting these enormous trees, measuring 150 to 200 feet in height, required a tremendous effort. Once the tree had been felled, which was no small task, it had to be pulled by a team of fifty to sixty oxen over miles of often unbroken forests to a river. From there it could be floated downstream until it reached the ocean and a specially designed mast ship. In all, New Hampshire supplied about 4,500 of these giant trees and gained a reputation for producing the finest masts in the world.

Goffstown, known for its fine timber, was at the center of this trade. During his early explorations up the Piscataquog River, John Goffe was amazed at the size of the white pine trees he saw on the pine plains on either side of the river. The town also served as the gateway to the fine white pine trees farther west and north, which were hauled down a road running parallel to the Piscataquog River—a road that still bears the name of its original purpose: Mast Road. It was undoubtedly cut by the teams of oxen bringing the massive logs to the Merrimack, although when it came into use is unknown. Likewise, when it became known as the Mast Road is unknown, although the name appears on a map as early as 1756.

The trade, however, produced a great deal of resentment among the colonists. Although supplying masts for the navy could be a profitable business for those lucky few who held special royal licenses as mast contractors, most colonists received almost nothing from the venture and, in fact, saw their best and largest trees taken by the government for very little compensation. In February 1772, this resentment came to a head

Ships of the line, such as the one depicted here, needed new masts every fifteen to twenty years, unless a storm or enemy action damaged them sooner.

when a deputy surveyor arrived in town and caught several residents at Job Dow's mill in the West Village trying to cut protected logs at the sawmill. The trees were confiscated and their owners fined, although an agent they hired to negotiate with the government managed to get the fine substantially reduced. Just over the Weare border in the village of Riverdale, though, the matter was not so peacefully resolved. There, a group of outraged settlers seized the deputy surveyor and his assistant in the middle of the night on April 14, 1772, and sent them fleeing from the town in an incident that has since become known as the Pine Tree Riot. This show of resistance did nothing to change the policy, though, or its enforcement in the Merrimack Valley.

Goffstown residents therefore had a local grievance to add to the larger disaffection between America and Britain. In Portsmouth, the leading figures of New Hampshire were finding themselves more and more at odds with Crown policies in a series of disputes that would push the province toward the overthrow of royal rule. In addition, many of the people of Goffstown had originally come from Massachusetts, the hotbed of colonial resistance, and continued to feel great sympathy and kinship with their families and neighbors to the south. It should come as no surprise then that when word of the Battle of Concord and Lexington reached Goffstown in the early morning of April 20, 1775—the day after the battle had been fought in Massachusetts—the residents met the news with immediate offers of assistance. By the following day, a company of militia from the Merrimack Valley, which included six men from Goffstown, had formed to march to Massachusetts to give what support it could. Only a few days later, another company formed that contained thirty-seven Goffstown men (more than half of its complement), and it also set off for Massachusetts. These troops were part of the force of two thousand New Hampshire men that traveled to Massachusetts in these first few weeks of the war to join with militias from all over New England in the siege around the British, who were ensconced in Boston.

On June 17, 1775, the New Hampshire men, formed into a regiment under General John Stark, played a pivotal role in the Battle of Bunker Hill, where they comprised two-thirds of the American force. Placed at a crucial spot in the American defenses on the left flank along a stone wall that ran from a redoubt to the Mystic River, the regiment turned back two assaults by the Welsh Fusiliers, one of the most formidable units in the British army. Before the second of these assaults, Stark ordered his men to hold their fire until the British were just fifty yards away, a command no doubt inspired by the fact that the men had been rationed just fifteen bullets each before the battle began. When Stark's troops did fire, the British line broke, with some Americans later declaring that the British soldiers had actually run away. The British troops were said to have fallen in such great numbers before the New Hampshire line that they covered the entire field "as thick as sheep in a fold," in the words of one British officer. The New Hampshire regiment, and indeed the entire American line, ultimately fell back after the third assault, with the New Hampshire men providing a covering fire for the orderly American retreat. The regiment suffered the second highest American losses of the day—sixty men killed or wounded, but only one of them was reportedly from Goffstown.

At no other single engagement of the war did so many Goffstown men serve than at Bunker Hill, but the battle proved the first in a long list of conflicts in which Goffstown troops fought throughout the war, all the way to the final showdown at Yorktown, Virginia, in 1781. Over the course of the war, 191 Goffstown men served in the military. That figure represents just about every able-bodied man in the town. A local tradition even credits

The Battle of Bunker Hill, in which New Hampshire men played such a crucial role.

one soldier, John Buswell or Buzwell, with serving as George Washington's bodyguard at Valley Forge in the winter of 1777–78. By war's end, eleven Goffstown men had been killed in the fighting.

Most of those from Goffstown who fought served in the militia rather than the Continental army, although army recruitments rose in the later years of the conflict. Militia troops had no uniforms, brought their own weapons and were fed and provisioned by their home colony, which requisitioned supplies from the towns. Militia enlistments were generally shorter, although many men reenlisted at least once. Continental army troops often received a bounty for signing up, their terms of service lasted at least a year and often three years, they received uniforms and weapons and their provisions were requisitioned by the Continental Congress, which still relied on individual colonies to raise the needed supplies.

Both forces, then, expected towns to send food and ammunition for the troops, which often placed incredible burdens on those at the homefront. The effort to supply the troops began immediately, starting with a special town meeting held on April 27, 1775, less than ten days after the British march on Concord and Lexington. For the duration of the war, Goffstown sent food, ammunition and other supplies to its soldiers serving in the militia; it sent large shipments of beef and grain to the Continental army; it paid for the bounties offered to those who enlisted in the army; it helped support the families of soldiers serving with either the militia or the army; and it relieved war widows of their tax burdens, as well as continuing to supply them with material aid for their farms.

Goffstown residents were also involved in furthering the political revolution that was occurring in New Hampshire with the overthrow of the royal government and the establishment of a new state government. Within days of Concord and Lexington, New Hampshire political figures called for a convention of town delegates to be held at Exeter in the spring and summer of 1775. This body replaced the old colonial legislature and eventually evolved into the New Hampshire General Court when New Hampshire became the first colony to declare itself a state. Hillsborough County also held a series of political conventions in 1774 and 1775 that met in Amherst to provide political leadership as the old colonial system broke down. Goffstown sent delegates to nearly all of these meetings, usually asking Moses Kelley, Samuel Blodget or John Goffe to represent them.

Moses Kelley was a particularly busy man during the Revolutionary War years. Not only was he a political figure, but he was also a militia captain and the head of the local chapter of the Sons of Liberty. No one knows when Goffstown's Sons of Liberty began meeting, but by the mid-1770s the group had become well established in town. They met on a regular basis at a tavern in Goffstown Center or at Kelley's tavern on Mast Road in the area known today as Pinardville. Kelley's tavern became the site of the one recorded incident of Tory violence that occurred in the area during the Revolution. Its target was Bedford's Presbyterian minister John Houston. Appointed to the town's ministry in 1756, Houston had long been a contentious figure in Bedford. When in March 1776 the New Hampshire Committee of Safety (which governed the colony throughout much of the war) called on all male residents to take an oath, known as the Association Oath, pledging their support for the war, Houston was the one man in the area to refuse. He was even known to have served guests such unpatriotic drinks as tea, a sure sign of loyalty to the British Crown. Sometime in May 1776, a group of Bedford and Goffstown men snatched Houston from his home, took him to Kelley's tavern, roughed him up a bit and paraded him around over roughly six miles "riding on a rail"—an old practice whereby the victim is forced to balance on a log while being hauled around and heckled by the perpetrators. No lasting damage was done or intended (the ruffians had promised Houston's wife they would bring him back unharmed), but Houston lost his position as Bedford's minister shortly thereafter.

Such light-hearted raillery (for everyone except Houston, that is) must have been a welcome reprieve from what was otherwise a grim picture during the war years, with many men gone to fight and the town's resources stretched thin. The few civic projects Goffstown had underway before the war started—mainly the effort to find a new minister and to hire a schoolmaster—were put on hold as all available money went instead to buy flint, lead and gunpowder for the troops.

The war years were also a period of political tension in town. Like most towns in New England, Goffstown had a committee of safety during the American Revolution. This group, composed of three selectmen and three other townsmen, literally governed the town during the course of the war, in effect replacing the selectmen as the town's governing body. The committee of safety was responsible for not only running the town but also getting supplies to the troops and ensuring that all the town's residents were loyal to the American cause. This last charge gave them a great deal of power over the lives of the townspeople. For example, in 1778 or 1779, this committee investigated whether every man in town was doing all he could to support the war effort, from serving in the militia to providing supplies for the troops and supporting their families to showing enough patriotic fervor. It was a power that could easily have been abused if committee of safety members had old scores to settle in town. If that happened in Goffstown, there does not appear to be a record of it, although any records would most likely have been colored and perhaps even distorted by patriotic fervor.

Such political and military turmoil also led to economic disturbances. Goffstown, like other New Hampshire communities during the war, reverted to a barter economy, as inflation made all currency valueless except silver, which was practically nonexistent. By the end of the war, the town's financial resources were nearly exhausted, ushering in a period of deep economic depression.

THE ENTERPRISING
SAMUEL BLODGET

E conomic prosperity did not begin to return to Goffstown and New Hampshire until the very end of the 1780s, but when it did a new spirit seemed to have taken hold. With the birth of the new nation, Americans embraced innovation and experimentation as never before, almost as if their liberation from British rule had prompted them to create themselves anew.

In the Merrimack Valley, that spirit was best personified by a visionary named Samuel Blodget, who recognized the potential of Amoskeag Falls to become a center of trade and industry. Born in 1724 in Woburn, Massachusetts, Blodget arrived in the area in 1751, buying a farm in Goffstown on the banks of the Merrimack River. He was a merchant and trader who produced potash (the processed ashes of trees used in the making of soap and glass) with great success. In 1757, he accompanied John Goffe's men on campaign and was present at the massacre that followed the surrender of Fort William Henry, when Indians (allied with the French) killed British and American troops and civilians as they left the fort after turning it over to the French. Although he lost all of his goods and even the clothes off his back, Blodget was one of those who managed to escape, hiking naked fifteen miles through the wilderness to British-held Fort Edwards.

Back home in New Hampshire after the war, Blodget threw himself into Goffstown affairs, particularly after the town was incorporated in 1761. His name frequently appears in the town records from the 1760s through the

This portrait is a highly idealized nineteenth-century view of Samuel Blodget, whom contemporaries described as a short, stocky man.

1790s, and he often held positions of some prestige in the town. It was Blodget who served as agent for the Goffstown lumber owners who were fined for cutting down white pine trees in 1772 and negotiated a settlement for them. Perhaps not coincidentally, he was appointed to the lucrative post of deputy surveyor of the woods shortly thereafter. In 1765, with his business interests thriving after he opened the first general store in Goffstown in the village of Amoskeag, he purchased additional tracts of land along both banks of the Merrimack River, investing heavily, and profitably, in the lumber trade. After the American Revolution, he spent four years in Europe promoting some of his inventions, but by the early 1790s he had returned home, determined to embark on a project that would become the great quest of his life: building a canal along the Merrimack River.

Even before the Revolutionary War, Blodget had envisioned a canal along the Merrimack so that boats could reach all the way up the river to Concord, which would allow him to capitalize on his lumber business, as well as present opportunities for all types of trade. But the war and his other projects intervened, and it wasn't until 1793 that his interest in the idea was reawakened. His renewed attention was probably sparked by news that a group of investors was building a canal in Massachusetts that would link the Merrimack River near East Chelmsford (the village that would later become the town of Lowell) with Boston Harbor in what became known as the Middlesex Canal.

Investing his own fortune in his canal project, Blodget ordered construction to begin on May 2, 1794. For the next thirteen years, the project would consume him and nearly all of his money. The canal was located on the east bank of the Merrimack River and was designed using a system of Blodget's own devising. The idea was that the canal would be constructed with a series of small reservoirs separated by gates. Boats would be propelled through the canal by the velocity of the water, which would accumulate in the reservoirs and then gently push the boats through the check gates. The problem lay in the fact that the angle of the slope through the canal was too steep; hence the velocity was too strong, and the boats were hurled through the check gates at speeds that threatened the boats and their cargoes. By 1797, the design flaw had become apparent to Blodget. To correct it, he designed two great locks to control the level of the water and allow the boats to circumvent the falls safely. Again, the design proved a failure, and the whole project nearly collapsed when a massive spring freshet in 1798 destroyed all of the mechanisms Blodget had created.

Chastened but not defeated, Blodget vowed to rebuild the canal, although he had nearly exhausted his own fortune, having spent close to $40,000 on the project thus far. He also recognized the problems inherent in his designs and vowed to employ more traditional technology for the locks and canal. In late 1799, he convinced the New Hampshire state legislature to allow him to run a lottery to raise funds for the project, an effort that produced another $5,000 for the venture, and he raised an additional $7,000 by selling stock in his canal company. Even Massachusetts allowed him to run lotteries for the project, believing that the canal would generate more business for its merchants. Both states permitted Blodget to run several lotteries over the next few years, which provided the capital he needed to finish the project by the very end of December 1806. On May 1, 1807, Blodget organized a grand celebration to mark the canal's opening. With the completion of the Middlesex Canal in 1802 and Blodget's Canal in 1807, boats could pass all the way from Concord to Boston unimpeded. Such a trip took four or five days depending on the direction traveled, significantly faster than going by road. Blodget's Canal also drastically reduced the cost of shipping goods to Concord to just one-fifth of the price. This difference proved of tremendous significance for the people living above the falls and allowed the town of Concord to grow more rapidly than it would otherwise have done.

Blodget's vision for the future did not stop there, however. Throughout the 1790s and the first decade of the 1800s, Blodget bought huge tracts of land on both sides of the Merrimack in Goffstown and Derryfield. In the short

A painting of Samuel Blodget's Manchester home (built in 1793) with Amoskeag Falls in the background and the canal in the foreground.

term, he hoped to earn a profit from the timber on this land, but in the long term he foresaw the land as vitally important to the region's future. While the canal was being built, Blodget had ordered the construction of a basin in the river that could be used as a source to generate hydraulic power. He already owned several gristmills and sawmills in the area, and his experiences with his failed designs for the canal had most likely impressed him with the power of the river itself, which had three significant drops within a half mile at Amoskeag Falls. Blodget became convinced that the Merrimack Valley would one day be a mighty industrial center, reportedly saying, "I see a city on the banks of the Merrimack, by these falls—a city that shall be the equal of the great manufacturing city of Manchester, England." So convinced was he that he purchased strips of land to the north of Amoskeag Falls specifically because of their deposits of natural clay, a vital component in the production of bricks, which would be used to build the new city.

For these reasons, and because Blodget built himself a large, comfortable home on the east side of the river in the 1790s, Manchester often claims Blodget as one of its own, although he lived in Goffstown much longer. When he died on September 1, 1807, just four months after the opening of his canal, the entire region felt his loss. In deference to his honor, the residents of Derryfield changed the town's name to Manchester just three years later.

GOFFSTOWN BRINGS MILLS
TO THE MERRIMACK

Samuel Blodget's faith in the Merrimack's industrial promise was quickly realized. Just three years after his death, the first textile mill was established on the river, on its west bank in the tiny village of Amoskeag in Goffstown. Although this mill experienced only modest success, it was the first mill of what became known as the Amoskeag Manufacturing Company, which would one day become the largest textile factory in the world.

Textile manufacturing appeared in the United States in 1789 and came to New Hampshire shortly thereafter, when the state's first woolen mill opened in New Ipswich, near the Massachusetts border, in 1801. New Ipswich also boasted the state's first cotton mill three years later. In 1808, one of the men who had started the New Ipswich mills, Benjamin Prichard, arrived in the Merrimack Valley and decided to build mills on the mighty river. His first efforts in Bedford proved unsuccessful, but in 1809, he entered into a partnership with three brothers—Ephraim, David and Robert Stevens—to build a mill on the west bank of the Merrimack near Amoskeag Falls. Needing capital for this business venture, the four men formed a corporation the following year that sold shares to local investors. Of the twenty original investors in the project, fourteen were from Goffstown, and the list of names included many of the town's most prominent citizens. They called the corporation the Amoskeag Cotton and

Woolen Manufacturing Company, and the mill opened its doors in the summer of 1810.

As was common of factory work in these early years of the nineteenth century, the production of finished cloth was only partly accomplished within the factory itself. The cotton, shipped straight from the slave fields of the South, had to be picked over by hand before it could be spun into yarn. This work was farmed out to local women who labored at the task in their homes, an arrangement known as the putting-out system. Wool also had to be carded (that is, the raw fibers must be brushed and separated to prepare them for spinning) in much the same way, although its sources were closer to home. The mill itself contained a spinning jenny, an English invention employing horse- or water-powered machinery to spin many skeins of thread simultaneously, whereas hand-operated spinning wheels could spin only one. Spinning the fibers into yarn was the only part of the process done in the factory. The spun yarn was sent back out to local women who used hand looms to weave the yarn into finished cloth. On average, these women earned three and a half cents per yard for woven cloth, and a decent weaver could produce ten to twelve yards per day. The yarn spun at the mill was such a valuable commodity that the women were paid in spools of it rather than in cash. They could use it to barter or trade for anything they needed. The arrival of the mills initially provided a much-needed additional source of revenue for struggling New Hampshire farmers.

The first few years of the mill's operation proved moderately successful, especially when the United States was at war with Britain between 1812 and 1815. The war dramatically reduced the flow of imported goods into the country, particularly woven cloth from British textile factories. The mill owners wisely reinvested their profits back into the business, buying some of the new machinery developed in Britain that had just begun to appear in America, such as the Arkwright spinning frame, which was an advanced version of the spinning jenny that produced better thread with even less labor. The Arkwright spinning frame employed at the Amoskeag mill was the first one in the state and represented a significant step forward for the state's textile industry.

Nevertheless, when the war ended in 1815 and trade was restored with Great Britain, the products of the British textile factories competed fiercely with those made by American mills, and the Amoskeag mill slipped into a slow decline. In 1819, the owners invested heavily in a power loom that replaced the women working in the countryside at their hand looms, and the mill began producing high-quality shirtings and sheetings, but the mill still did not bring in much return for its owners.

Transformations of a New England Town

In 1822, the Amoskeag Company was sold to a single individual, a machinist from England named Olney Robinson who had helped install some of the early machines at the mill. Robinson was a protégé of Samuel Slater, the man who had been responsible for bringing much of the British textile industry's technology to the United States, earning himself the sobriquet "the father of the American Industrial Revolution." During Robinson's brief tenure running the mill, he bought up what was left of Samuel Blodget's farm on the west bank of the river, as well as a large tract of property farther south owned by another enterprising Goffstown man, Robert McGregor. McGregor had built the first bridge over the Merrimack in 1792, and like his contemporary Blodget, he foresaw the great potential of the river for the area's development. But Robinson's tenure as the mill's owner was brief. In 1826, he sold the operation to Slater and a collection of other partners, most notably Oliver Dean, a doctor and manufacturer from Massachusetts.

Dean promptly moved to Amoskeag Village and took over the day-to-day operations of the mill with great vigor. That same year, the company built a second mill in Amoskeag Village known as the Bell Mill, so named because the bell in its steeple called the factory workers to their jobs every morning and released them every night. Three stories high and employing about twenty-five people at any one time, the Bell Mill served not only as a factory but also as a machine shop, allowing machinery to be created and repaired on site. Unlike the first mill, now called the Old Mill, the Bell Mill produced ticking—the case or covering for mattresses, particularly the feather or horsehair mattresses that were in common usage before the twentieth century. The ticking industry was so successful that shortly after the Bell Mill opened the Amoskeag Company built a third factory that became known as the Island Mill because of its location on an island in the middle of the Merrimack River. The islands in the Merrimack had once been part of Goffstown, but in 1825, just one year before the Island Mill was constructed, the islands were annexed by Manchester.

The Old Mill and the Bell Mill proved the making of Amoskeag Village on the west side of the river. The sleepy little hamlet emerged as a thriving, bustling community in the years after the first mill opened. As more workers and managers flocked to the area, boardinghouses and shops quickly went up, promising a new era of prosperity for the village in the late 1820s. In that decade, Amoskeag was the most well populated of Goffstown's villages. It also entertained some well-known visitors, as it was a convenient stopping place for those traveling to Concord. On June 25, 1825, the Amoskeag Inn hosted "the Nation's Guest," the Revolutionary War hero Marquis de Lafayette,

The Bell Mill, constructed in Amoskeag Village in 1826.

who was on a triumphal tour of New England during his one-year sojourn in the United States. He had been invited back to America by President James Monroe and the U.S. Congress so that Americans could express to him their gratitude and admiration. Eight years later, on June 28, 1833, the Amoskeag Inn hosted President Andrew Jackson while he also took a tour of New England. Included in his party was Vice President Martin Van Buren, who would become president himself after Jackson.

In 1831, the Amoskeag Manufacturing Company was incorporated with capital valued at $1 million, an enormous amount in those days. Dean remained the primary force behind the company's success and served as its first president. Under his direction, the company began buying up land on both sides of the river in earnest, preparing for a massive expansion that began in 1836. In that year, the company's new mills on the east side of the river were built, with funding from an expanded list of investors that included some of the most prominent names in the New England textile industry, including the men who had started the mills at Lowell and Lawrence, Massachusetts. Indeed, nearly all of the new investors were from Massachusetts, and they brought with them big plans and large amounts of capital.

Transformations of a New England Town

It was at this point that the Manchester mills began to develop into the complex of industrial efficiency that allowed them to grow so dramatically throughout the nineteenth and early twentieth centuries. The days of local women taking piecework into their homes to produce cloth were long over. Instead, the company either bought or made massive amounts of new equipment, all powered by the Merrimack River, that allowed them to produce finished cloth within the factory, relying only on relatively inexpensive laborers, who came first from the surrounding countryside and then from across the Atlantic. As the mills grew, the factories and the town of Manchester expanded across the undeveloped land along the east side of the river. Surprisingly, very little of this development spilled over into Amoskeag Village. Instead, the Old Mill, the Bell Mill and the Island Mill were slowly replaced by newer, more efficient mills farther south on the east bank of the Merrimack below Amoskeag Falls. The Island Mill burned down in 1840, and the Bell Mill and Old Mill did the same in 1847.

By then, the Amoskeag Manufacturing Company was well on its way to becoming one of the largest industries in the United States, and the small village of Derryfield had transformed into the multiethnic, bustling city of Manchester. Between the 1830 and 1840 census, Manchester's population skyrocketed from just 877 people in 1830 to 3,235 in 1840. Manchester's population thus surpassed Goffstown's (which stood at 2,376 in 1840) for the first time in a reversal of the two communities' relative size that remains today. By 1850, Manchester's population had risen dramatically again to nearly 14,000 people, a phenomenal rate of growth in just two decades. The people living in the portion of Goffstown that lay on the west bank of the Merrimack River found that they had more in common with industrial Manchester than with the still predominantly agricultural community of Goffstown. In 1853, Manchester annexed that part of Goffstown, composed of about four thousand acres of land, and another strip of land to the south owned by Bedford and containing the village of Piscataquog. Many Goffstown residents were angry and upset over Manchester's acquisition, but the city's increasing power and influence at the state level prohibited any effective protest from being lodged against the annexation. With this change, Goffstown settled into the boundaries it has today and relinquished its hold on the Amoskeag Manufacturing Company.

GOFFSTOWN EMBRACES THE IDEA OF "TOWNSHIP"

The riverfront was not the only place changing in the early nineteenth century. The countryside was changing as well, and changing dramatically. The frontier settlement that had been Goffstown before the American Revolution began to take on a more settled feel in the decades after the war. The town started to develop the services and social organizations that would create stronger bonds among the townspeople. The disparate farms and settlements of the colonial era gave way to the commercial areas and school districts of an established town. These social changes were predicated on economic changes—primarily shifts in agricultural production and the rise of the Industrial Revolution.

By the early decades of the nineteenth century, the agricultural subsistence economy of the eighteenth century was increasingly being replaced by a more specialized and yet more diverse economic structure that affected even traditional farming. The New England farm had always been a highly diversified operation. Unlike agriculture in the South that relied on just a handful of cash crops like tobacco, rice and cotton, New England agriculture produced a much wider variety of products. The typical farm in colonial New England grew crops such as wheat, corn, rye, grass, potatoes or hops; it kept livestock for labor, meat and a variety of animal products such as leather and milk; it contained wood lots that produced lumber; it maintained stores of fish and furs; it produced specialty items like apples, blueberries and maple sugar; it converted ash from its timber operations, as well as from household fires, into potash and pearl ash for the manufacturing of soap and glass; and it created a broad range of home crafts like furniture, cloth, barrels, ironworks and anything else that could be produced by hand on a small scale. For some, these home crafts became substantial businesses unto themselves. Goffstown's own John Dunlap, who lived in town before the American Revolution, became one of the most noted cabinetmakers in eighteenth-century America. He crafted much of this furniture while he ran a farm in Goffstown. For most farmers, though, these enterprises generated enough income to maintain their families with just a little bit left over to sell or barter for items they did not produce themselves.

There was not much margin for error or misfortune. The death of the head of the family, or a lack of children who could work on the farm, usually spelled disaster. Even some of the leading figures in a community could find themselves paupers because of a sudden reversal. This fate befell one of Goffstown's town fathers, James Karr, the man whose barn had once housed

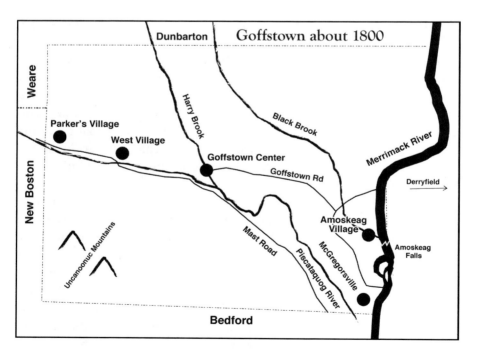

Goffstown in 1800 had several small villages, but most of the settlements were scattered farms around the town. There were very few roads or other amenities, like schools or churches. *Map created by Marshall Hudson.*

town meetings and who had donated land for the construction of the town's meetinghouse in 1768. By 1805, Karr had gone bankrupt and petitioned to become a charge on the town. Widows were in a particularly precarious position, as evidenced by the disproportionate numbers of them listed on the town's poor rolls, beginning in 1774 with the widow Elizabeth Dommorin, Goffstown's first pauper.

Each town was responsible for providing its own poor relief and generally followed the same procedure. Those people who believed they could no longer survive without material assistance would throw themselves upon the mercy of the town. If the person was from the town, which could be interpreted as either being born there or having lived there for an extended period (depending on the stance adopted by the selectmen), the town would subject the pauper to a rigorous examination to ensure that there were no other alternatives to town relief. Paupers from other towns would be sent back to their original town in an arrangement known as the warning-out system, which was widely employed throughout New England until the mid-nineteenth century. If the selectmen came to the decision that relief was merited and necessary, they then had to decide what level of relief to grant. In some cases, the town simply contributed food or material assistance. But in more extreme cases, when the pauper's debts were so high that his land had to be sold, the pauper would be rented out to another family in town to work as an indentured servant, with the town contributing to the person's upkeep. It was a brutal system that split up families. The care of children, who were also farmed out as indentured servants even at very young ages, was left to the selectmen, the parents being considered incapable of exercising good judgment in the matter.

In 1823, Goffstown built a poor farm, which allowed the indigent to sleep and eat in one central location, although they were still sent out to work on farms around town during the day. The poor farm also housed petty criminals and a whole list of social deviants, including "rogues, vagabonds, common beggars, lude [lewd] or disorderly persons" and the mentally ill. Although everyone who was able to work was rented out in the community, the poorhouse was not self-supporting, so its residents still required financial assistance from the townspeople. Usually, the poorhouse had a population of seven to ten inmates, many of them elderly. It was not until 1849 that the county took over poor relief and constructed a countywide poorhouse on land in Goffstown. The county poorhouse was a workhouse, employing paupers in manual labor jobs that nobody else wanted. Being sent to the workhouse was considered the worst fate that could befall someone, and most people went to great lengths to avoid it. On the same parcel of land, the county also constructed a hospital and a jail. The new county facility was located on Mast Road near the center of town, on three hundred acres that had been owned by Noyes Poor—the same piece of land where the county complex stands today.

The dramatic changes in farming in the early and mid-nineteenth century did not substantially lessen the vulnerability of widows and orphans to the threat of a life of poverty, although the establishment of the mills offered women and children opportunities for employment that could save many of them from the poorhouse. In these early years of industrialization, the mills were not viewed as competition to agricultural life but as a supplement to it, since farmers provided the textile factories with two desperately needed resources: labor and wool.

The labor was supplied by young people from the surrounding countryside, particularly young women who outnumbered men in the factories by a ratio of about three to one in the 1830s and 1840s. Although men did work in the factories, women proved the best laboring force for these ventures. First, there was a surplus of young women in the countryside since their farm productivity was lower than that of their brothers. Second, because their income was considered supplemental for a family and not the primary income, women were willing to accept lower wages. And third, women, with their smaller fingers and greater care for delicate work, proved more adept at working with textiles than men. The vast majority of the factory workers, both men and women, came from farms immediately in the vicinity of Manchester, specifically Goffstown, Bedford, Hooksett and Auburn, particularly in the early years of the mills' operation, when only one hundred or so people worked in the factories. By the early 1840s, when the workforce at the mills started to number closer to one thousand people, more workers started coming in from out of state, most notably Massachusetts. It wasn't until the late 1840s that New England mill girls, as they were called, were displaced by a wave of foreign immigration, particularly Irish immigration, prompting them to leave their manufacturing jobs in large numbers.

The other resource supplied by New England farmers was wool. Sufficient quantities of cotton were shipped in from the South to keep the factories humming, but wool was a different matter. Beginning in the 1810s, when Merino sheep began to be imported from Spain and Portugal, New Hampshire farmers discovered that sheep were a far more suitable commodity for their rocky, hilly landscape than growing traditional crops.

Transformations of a New England Town

The sheep seemed unaffected by the acidic soil, the inclement weather and the short growing season. And with textile mills springing up all over New England, there was a ready market that was easily accessible for their product. By 1830, the sheep industry had nearly taken over New Hampshire farming, so much so that the governor of New Hampshire declared in 1836 that the people of Hillsborough County no longer grew enough food to support themselves.

Goffstown farmers participated in this boom, abandoning their usual crops and turning their fields into pastures, which was not an easy transition. To switch from growing crops to raising significant numbers of sheep, more land had to be cleared and larger pastures had to be created. All of these pastures had to be surrounded by stone walls, which originally stood three to four feet high and were constructed by the farmers themselves. In 1836, at the height of the great sheep boom in New Hampshire, Goffstown farmers kept over 1,400 head, a tremendous number considering that before the sheep boom, the town probably contained no more than 200 sheep. Other towns in Hillsborough County were greater sheep producers, though, and the county as a whole raised far fewer sheep than did farmers in the Connecticut River Valley. In that same boom year, the state contained close to half a million head of sheep, providing wool to more than one hundred textile factories in New England. Goffstown farmers may not have been major wool producers when compared to the rest of the state, but sheep raising represented a significant shift in their agricultural practices and one that would remain for several decades. In 1850, the town still had over 900 sheep and produced more than three thousand pounds of wool per year.

Industrialization also encouraged the rise of a more commercial society, in which manufactured goods were available in greater quantities and at lower prices than ever before, prompting a demand for more merchants, shops and commercial centers. The little villages that dotted the township, which in the eighteenth century had contained possibly a church, burying ground or maybe an inn or tavern, started to become business centers with stores and restaurants. William Parker's store, which opened in 1804 at Parker's Village, a small but thriving settlement near the New Boston–Weare line, is an example of this new commercialism.

The need to transport goods also became more important, prompting the construction of roads and the creation of early forms of mass transport. In Goffstown, these improvements had been a long time coming, as the state government cited the town for the poor condition of its roads—and its lack of roads altogether—in 1810, the first of many such citations for Goffstown. Nevertheless, the town did undertake the expensive task of improving its road system, building over the next several decades Wallace Road (1820), the extension of Goffstown Road (commonly known now as the Back Road) along the north side of the river between Goffstown Center (Grasmere) and the West Village (1841), and transforming what had been nothing more than Indian trails or bridle paths into actual roads all over the town. Goffstown also invested in road improvements or new roads to the surrounding towns of Dunbarton, Weare and New Boston. Traveling by road was still slow and treacherous, though. A trip to Boston in the winter, traveling by sled, could easily take twelve days each way—hence the frequency of small inns and taverns at crossroads to provide shelter for travelers on their long journeys. Stagecoaches began to operate through the town as well, mostly running parallel to the Merrimack River through the villages of McGregorsville and Amoskeag and along Mast Road. By far the easiest and quickest way to travel was by water, and several enterprising men operated ferry services or boat transportation on the Merrimack. The shallowness of the Piscataquog, as well as its frequent falls and rapids, meant that it was not navigable. Boats also could not operate in the winter when the rivers froze, limiting their usefulness.

Inevitably, economic change brought social change as well. As in the eighteenth century, religion remained of great importance in most people's lives, but some of the denominational schisms that had so plagued the community in the years shortly after its settlement had subsided. After more than twenty-five years of tension between the Congregationalists and the Presbyterians, they finally joined together in a brief show of unanimity when they formed the Presbyterian Congregational Church in December 1801. The impetus for such a union was their mutual agreement to hire a young doctor turned preacher named David Lawrence Morril as the town's minister. Unlike the town's first minister, Joseph Currier, Morril proved a serious man who generally disapproved of the townspeople's tendency for revelry and dancing over prayer and reflection. He was one of a new breed of ministers who had been preaching in New Hampshire with greater frequency since the American Revolution. They were called the New Divinity, and they advocated a more personal, emotional connection to God than had the Harvard-educated ministers who predominated in the clergy for much of the eighteenth century with their more intellectual approach to religion. In a more extreme form, this new type of worship had already gained a foothold with other denominations, particularly the Baptists, who

HON. DAVID L. MORRIL

Goffstown's minister in the early nineteenth century, David L. Morril. Morril generally disapproved of how much Goffstown residents drank and danced, preferring to spend his time in sober reflection on the state of his soul.

encouraged parishioners to express their emotional fervor during church services with tears, fits and screaming. The Congregationalists and the Presbyterians frowned on such behavior, but they did feel some sympathy for the idea that God's grace should have a palpable effect on people, touching each person individually.

Morril embodied this idea and seemed to relish the opportunity to discuss with his parishioners the state of their souls, writing in his diary, "I would talk [about religion] from morning till night without cessation." During his years as the minister of Goffstown, he recorded in his diary conversation after conversation in which he tried to impress upon people the need to embrace a stronger, more emotional faith. On an early visit to Goffstown shortly before he accepted the pastoral position, he wrote that while staying at Enoch Page's he "had a good opportunity to converse with them [some ladies from the town], which I gladly improved. Some of them wept, & none of them appeared indifferent. I spent the whole time in conversation with them upon their danger & the necessity of personal religion." Morril viewed such strong signs of emotionalism among his future flock as a promising sign.

David L. Morril's Goffstown home from 1802 until 1831. *Courtesy of the Goffstown Historical Society, Snay Collection.*

The earnest young minister proved too much for the Presbyterians, though, who ended the union in 1806. Instead, the Presbyterians returned to the church in Bedford, where their faith was predominant. Morril remained the town minister (albeit only for the Congregationalists) until 1811, when he decided to rededicate himself to medicine. He continued to live in Goffstown for another twenty years, during which time he became a major political figure in the state, serving in the U.S. Senate and as governor of New Hampshire.

The New Divinity movement's emphasis on personal religion led to a statewide reexamination of the law that linked church and state in New Hampshire. Personal religion implied that all individuals must be free to follow their own personal conscience, thus undermining the idea of an established church. Therefore, in 1819, the law was revoked, meaning that towns could no longer tax their residents to support a minister. The New Divinity movement eventually merged with a larger religious trend sweeping across the country in the 1810s and 1820s, the Second Great Awakening, which dramatically increased church membership and provided a strong social component to religion. Simply put, the Second Great Awakening advocated that good Christians must work for a greater good in society, touching off a wave of reform movements and civic activism.

The churches themselves witnessed the spread of new denominations in town, such as the Universalist Society (established in 1822). Other groups formed as support organizations for existing denominations, including the Religious Union Society (established by Congregationalists in 1816) and the Goffstown Liberal Society (established by Methodists in 1841). The number of churches in town rose as well, with the Baptists and Methodists constructing their own facilities and the Congregationalists building a second church in the West Village. For the Baptists and the Methodists, the construction of their own town churches meant they no longer had to travel to other towns, like Dunbarton or Bow, for services, another factor that emphasized their connection to Goffstown.

All of these churches experienced religious revivals during these years—some small and others more substantial. These experiences increased membership and a sense of social responsibility among the participants, strengthening the bonds of community and encouraging civic engagement. The Congregational Church had already begun to formalize its role as a provider of social services, opening a Sabbath school in 1822.

In Goffstown, these trends became apparent in a variety of ways. One of the most popular reform efforts in town focused on education, as more money and attention began to be paid to the community's underfunded school system. Town residents also began showing greater concern for the underprivileged—hence the construction of the poor farm in 1823 and the banning of corporal punishment there in 1828. Another major reform effort in town was temperance, a movement spearheaded by the Congregationalist minister Henry Wood beginning in 1826. Although the campaign to ban the use of alcohol, particularly at public functions like burials and weddings, collapsed after Wood completed his five-year appointment and moved on, it resurfaced roughly twenty years later when the town voted to go dry in 1853.

There is curiously little in the historical record regarding the single most powerful reform movement of its day: the antislavery movement. And yet it was a vital organization in Goffstown, with a membership of 160 people in 1837 at the height of the movement, which represented nearly a seventh of the town's adult population. The group was started in April 1835 by thirty-five Goffstown residents. An auxiliary organization to the American Anti-Slavery Society, it was founded during the early months of the antislavery movement's initiation in New Hampshire. The state antislavery society had formed in November of the previous year, and by

May 1835 only about a dozen other communities in New Hampshire had local organizations, making Goffstown's among the first in the state. By the end of 1837, New Hampshire had about seventy antislavery societies, with roughly 4,500 members statewide. If the organization were similar to other antislavery groups in New Hampshire, it would have participated in the petition campaign, when local groups gathered thousands of signatures on petitions asking the U.S. Congress to abolish slavery. When Congress tabled the petitions without a hearing, fearing that the issue of slavery was too divisive to be considered, thousands of additional northerners objected, believing a southern conspiracy was operating in the federal government to deprive them of their constitutional rights—in this case, the right to petition their representatives. It was one of the most successful tactics of the antislavery groups and made thousands of people in the North more sympathetic to their cause than otherwise would have been. Local antislavery groups also sponsored lectures and circulated antislavery books and pamphlets. There is no doubt that antislavery sentiment was strong in this region of New Hampshire. Some sources even claim that the ex-slave Frederick Douglass wrote his famous autobiography detailing his life in slavery while staying with a Quaker family in nearby Weare.

Not everyone in town endorsed these sentiments, though, despite the large numbers who joined the local antislavery society. In the decades before the Civil War, the Underground Railroad apparently came through Goffstown, meaning that there were safe houses in town in which runaway slaves could hide while making their journey to Canada. Local lore has it that when word got out about the location of a safe house, the owner was often tarred and feathered by a group of local ruffians, evidence of a time when local law enforcement was a matter of residents acting of their own accord.

There was also an explosion in the number of civic organizations in town, which had as their goal the improvement of the town itself and its residents. For example, in the year 1827 alone, Goffstown witnessed the creation of a corporation to establish a library (Goffstown Union Library) and a fire company (Amoskeag Fire Company No. 1), as well as the founding of a Masonic chapter (Bible Lodge No. 27). All types of groups sprang up, from sewing bees to literary societies. By 1856, the town even had a musical group, the Goffstown Cornet Band.

The result of all these efforts was a new sense of "township." In the eighteenth century, Goffstown had contained a scattering of farms, clustered around crossroads and in family groups. There had been little sense of belonging to a larger community—a "town." Other ties in the

Merrimack Valley had been stronger: to family, to friends, to those of the same religion and to people they had known before coming to New Hampshire. These ties had transcended town boundaries and linked the residents of Goffstown, Bedford, Derryfield, Dunbarton, New Boston, Weare and other communities in a network of relationships but not to any specific place. All that changed in the years after the American Revolution. In the first half of the nineteenth century, each of these towns saw the development of the kinds of infrastructure (roads, schools, businesses and commercial centers) and civic organizations (church groups, poorhouses, libraries, reform societies and fire companies) that would help define the idea of the town and encourage the residents to identify more closely with their fellow townspeople.

The townspeople's newfound sense of community also encountered challenges during these years, most seriously with the rise of various movements to divide the township into several different towns or to annex part of Goffstown to the surrounding communities. The most notable efforts came in 1814, 1840, 1853 and 1858. Some came dangerously close

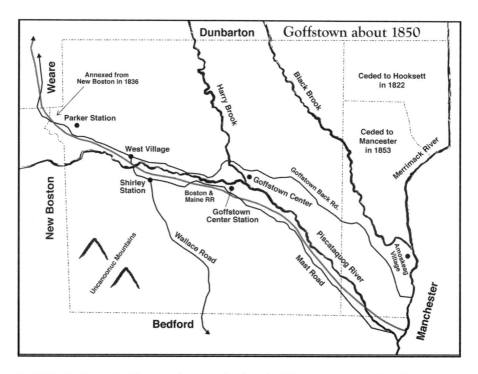

By 1850, Goffstown had become far more developed, with many more roads and even a railroad. *Map created by Marshall Hudson.*

to succeeding, and one actually did—Manchester's annexation of eastern Goffstown in 1853. All of the attempts to divide the town were along geographic lines. They illustrated the townspeople's growing identification with one another, at least with their neighbors, if not with the town as a whole. And yet the fact that nearly every attempt failed shows that many people in Goffstown did have a sense of township that transcended the bonds of individual villages.

In all of these movements, Goffstown mirrored trends occurring at the state and regional level. The town's experiences were in many ways typical of that of other towns in New Hampshire at this time, although there was more industry in Goffstown than in most New Hampshire communities. One episode in this period stood out dramatically, though, and made Goffstown the center of attention, albeit briefly. Unfortunately, it was not the kind of attention any town would want.

MURDER!

G offstown did not become the center of attention for its accomplishments but for the worst possible reason: crime, and more specifically, murder. In 1821, a young day laborer named Daniel Davis Farmer beat to death the widow Anna Ayer on her Goffstown farm, sparking a wave of public attention that turned all eyes to Goffstown as Farmer was captured, tried and executed.

Many of the details of Ayer's murder remain unknown. What little information there is comes from the trial transcript and Farmer's own testimonial. Penned while he was in jail between the time of his sentencing and his execution, the *Life and Confessions of Daniel Davis Farmer* was published as a pamphlet when he died and quickly sold out two editions. Indeed, newspaper accounts of his death also contain advertisements for his testimonial.

Not much is known about the widow Ayer, and by Farmer's own account there seemed to be little of note in his own life before this incident. As a youth, he had worked as a laborer at various farms in Goffstown, including Ayer's. He eventually bought his own small parcel of land, married, had children and then moved to Manchester, from where he originally came. He continued to keep in touch with several of his former employers in Goffstown and to hire himself out to them to earn extra money.

Farmer claimed that his troubles began in the summer of 1820 with a minor financial dispute between himself and the widow over his labor, involving a field of grass he was supposed to cut for her. He had originally agreed to cut it but then refused the job when he found out how little she was prepared to pay for his services. About six months later, in January 1821, Ayer publicly named Farmer as the father of her unborn child when pressed by Goffstown selectmen to assign blame for her rumored condition. Ayer was already receiving financial support from the town, and unless paternity could be established for the coming baby, the town would be compelled to pay for its birth, care and rearing. Although Farmer vehemently denied the charge, he was told by others in town that Ayer's word would carry the day at a paternity trial, despite what he refers to as her generally acknowledged "low character." The mere accusation itself had cost Farmer money for bail that he could ill afford, forcing him to take out a loan. Farmer wrote that in desperation, he went to Ayer's house on the night of April 4, 1821, to try to get some straight answers from her. He took with him a bottle of rum, of which she was apparently fond. They talked by her fire and drank rum for some time, while Ayer's teenaged daughter sat nearby and listened. Finally, as Farmer prepared to leave, Ayer walked with him onto the front porch, and he asked Ayer about the pending paternity trial. The story that Ayer told him made his blood boil.

Ayer admitted to him candidly that the child belonged to another man, even telling Farmer the man's name. Farmer himself did not repeat the man's name in his testimonial, stating that his silence was in deference to the feelings of the man's family and friends. The only clues Farmer provided were that the man lived near Ayer and that he had a fierce temper. Whoever he was, he reportedly forced Ayer to keep quiet and put her in fear for her life. Even then, after telling all this to Farmer, she refused to his face to publicly recant her accusation against him. Farmer stated that "in an instant my passion was raised to a height beyond description; quick as thought snatching a club as she started to go into the house, I pursued, struck and beat her." He claimed to have no memory of hitting Ayer's daughter or of trying to set fire to the house, as the daughter later testified at the trial. He stated that he had not the faintest idea that he had beat the widow so badly as to kill her and even suggested that she would not have died from the beating if she hadn't already been so poor, and by implication, insufficiently cared for by the town. The widow died shortly thereafter, although her daughter recovered to testify against Farmer. He was captured without incident, arraigned on April 21 at a session of the county's superior court meeting in Hopkinton and detained in the jail at Amherst, the county seat, until his trial on October 10. In a single day, the court heard all the evidence, and arguments were made for and against the accusation. The jury returned with a guilty verdict shortly

The Amherst Congregational Church, where Farmer's trial was held. There were too many people in attendance to fit in the courthouse.

after eleven o'clock that same night. The next day, Judge Levi Woodbury pronounced the sentence of death, setting the date for December 22. The governor gave Farmer a brief reprieve, but he was hanged just two weeks later, on January 3, 1822, in Amherst.

The execution itself proved to be a massive public event. Despite bitterly cold temperatures, an estimated ten thousand people turned out to watch, more than five times the population of Amherst at the time. Capital punishment was still administered in public (and would be in New Hampshire until 1868), and execution days tended to take on an almost carnival-like atmosphere, no doubt prompted by their rarity. Whole families would take the day off from their activities to go and see a hanging, and vendors wandered the crowds selling food and other articles, including sometimes a pamphlet or broadside regarding the execution being carried out that day. New Hampshire executed just fifteen men in the nineteenth century and only four of them between 1800 and 1850. All of them had been convicted of murder if not some other crime in conjunction with it. Farmer's was perhaps the most widely publicized and garnered the most attention.

Farmer certainly earned the good opinion of the crowd, despite the crime that put him there. Witnesses reported that he seemed "composed and prayerful" throughout the proceedings, conduct that the crowd could not help but respect. He arrived at the gallows on a sleigh, which was followed by a second sleigh bearing his coffin. After mounting the scaffold, he gave a short speech (that does not seem to have been preserved) and then prayed briefly with the aptly named Reverend Nathan Lord of Amherst's Congregational church. After the noose was placed around his neck, Farmer let fall from his hand a handkerchief to signal that he was prepared, and the trapdoor beneath his feet was opened. He struggled briefly and then was still. After the surgeons declared him dead, his brother took his body back to Manchester for burial.

An interesting side note is the identity of the executioner: he was the sheriff of Amherst County, General Benjamin Pierce, the father of future U.S. president Franklin Pierce. As there were so few executions carried out, the sheriff was called upon to fulfill the role on this occasion since the county did not have a regular executioner. By all accounts, Pierce was horrified by the part he had to play in the proceedings. Witnesses claimed that he was as pale as Farmer himself in the moments before the hanging and that his hand shook badly when he reached for the lever that would release the drop.

The murder of the widow Ayer and the resulting execution of Daniel Davis Farmer brought Goffstown much unwanted attention, even though Farmer's reputation underwent something of a metamorphosis during this period. Immediately after the murder and in the months leading up to the trial, Farmer was portrayed as a low, shifty character who had committed a foul and inexcusable crime. But after he was sentenced to death, the media changed the way it depicted him. His story became, in essence, a cautionary tale. Increasingly, Farmer's history was viewed as tragic and he himself as a victim of one moment of bad judgment that cost two people their lives—the widow's and his own. This attitude was prevalent throughout the coverage during and after the execution, in newspapers, pamphlets and broadsides. In fact, one broadside included a poem to emphasize the message that read, in part:

> *Deluded man! reproach of human kind!*
> *Cut down in youth, to infamy consign'd!*
> *May all who read, ere fame or life be lost,*
> *Here learn experience cheaply at thy cost.*
>
> *Learn to restrain their passions, ere too late,*
> *And thus avoid thy misery and thy fate,*
> *Thus shall their lives flow smoothly to the end,*
> *With man's applause and heaven itself their friend.*

THE CIVIL WAR COMES TO GOFFSTOWN

Few events in American history have had the far-reaching impact of the Civil War, which historians generally view as the start of modern American history—the breaking point between its distant and recent past. The Civil War affected every facet of American society, as people committed themselves to the waging of war, whether they joined the army or worked at home to support the war effort. In many ways, Goffstown's experience during the war was typical of other towns in New Hampshire, although in 1864 the town would nearly experience a civil war of its own when residents almost came to blows at the town meeting. These hard, tense years took a heavy toll on the community, and when they were over, Goffstown, like the rest of the North, entered a new industrial era that would change the town in ways no one could foresee.

When the Civil War broke out in April 1861, New Hampshire no longer had a militia system from which to draw trained troops. In the decades after the American Revolution, the state's militias had become increasingly ineffective. Each town's yearly militia muster had degenerated into a public holiday, with the men conducting haphazard training exercises in the morning followed by mock battles that became general mêlées in the afternoon. Families would turn out en masse to watch the festivities, which always included prodigious amounts of drinking, eating, gambling and dancing. In fact, a huge fistfight erupted at the Goffstown muster of 1839,

The West Village about the time of the Civil War. *Courtesy of the Goffstown Historical Society, Snay Collection.*

Another photograph of Goffstown from about the time of the Civil War; this one is of the town's south common on the other side of the river. *Courtesy of the Goffstown Historical Society, Snay Collection.*

resulting in a man's death when he suffered a blow to the head. The town's last regular muster occurred in May 1850, and the state disbanded the militias the following year. In their place grew up private companies, which were really more like fraternal organizations than trained military bands. Goffstown had two in the 1850s: the Goffstown Light Infantry (from the western half of the town) and the Amoskeag Phalanx (from the eastern half). Both groups had uniforms, conducted exercises and engaged in a competitive rivalry with each other.

Just as had happened at the outbreak of the Revolutionary War, the Civil War sparked an immediate turnout of volunteers, eager to enlist and fight for the preservation of the Union. On April 13, 1861, one day after the attack occurred, the town received word of the Confederate bombardment of Fort Sumter in the harbor of Charleston, South Carolina. Three men from town immediately joined the newly established First Regiment of the New Hampshire Volunteer Infantry, signing up at one of the state's twenty-eight hastily erected recruitment centers. During the course of the war, New Hampshire raised eighteen regiments of infantry, and Goffstown men served in nearly all of them. They also served in New Hampshire heavy artillery and cavalry units, the units of other states (including Massachusetts, Rhode Island and Vermont) and the U.S. Navy. The largest concentration of Goffstown men was in the Second New Hampshire Volunteer Infantry Regiment and the Tenth New Hampshire Volunteer Infantry Regiment, both of which contained thirty-three men from the town.

The Second New Hampshire, mustered in early June 1861, served longer than any other regiment from New Hampshire, fighting for nearly the entire course of the war in some of the fiercest battles, from First Bull Run in July 1861 to the fall of the Confederate capitol of Richmond in April 1865. Part of the Union's Army of the Potomac, the regiment spent nearly the entire war fighting in Virginia. Of the many battles it participated in, it suffered the heaviest casualties in the Battle of Gettysburg on July 1–3, 1863, when the unit lost roughly 60 percent of its men on the second day of the engagement (only one Goffstown man from the regiment was killed in this battle). The regiment also participated in the Battle of Cold Harbor in early June 1864, when Union troops hurled themselves in a frontal attack against Confederate entrenchments covering Richmond. The assault proved an abysmal failure, and the Second New Hampshire was among the many Federal regiments to sustain substantial casualties, although none from Goffstown.

The Tenth New Hampshire saw far less action, although it was also part of the Army of the Potomac and spent most of its service in Virginia.

Mustered in early September 1862, the regiment served until June 1865, participating in a string of battles that included Fredericksburg and Cold Harbor, where two Goffstown men from the regiment were killed. More Goffstown men died while serving in the Tenth New Hampshire than any other regiment—seven men, or roughly one-fifth of the Goffstown men who had enlisted in the regiment.

Over the course of the war, a total of 192 men from Goffstown enlisted in the Federal army, of whom 31 were killed in action or died of disease. Another 31 men were wounded. The numbers might seem small when compared with the staggering Union losses during the war, but their effect on the town was significant, particularly as the adult population was fewer than 1,000 people in 1860. Throughout the course of the war, 40 percent of the adult male population were in the military; 14 percent were killed or wounded.

Even for those who remained at home, the war's effects were tremendous. They affected nearly every aspect of town life. From the earliest days of the war, the towns of New Hampshire played a vital role in supplying the troops, as each town was expected to contribute provisions to the state for the support of its soldiers. Women formed ladies' auxiliary societies to sew uniforms and make bandages. The town deployed its funds to buy guns, ammunition, knapsacks, bedrolls and other necessary supplies for the troops, as well as sending food and alcohol rations. Many towns also offered bounties to enlisting men: Goffstown initially offered those who volunteered for military service a bonus of $125. By the end of the war, when able-bodied men were becoming scarce, the town's bounty had increased to $600 as Goffstown, like other communities, struggled to meet the quota for soldiers imposed by the state. The town also gave support for soldiers' families, although the soldiers were expected to send most of their $13 per month of pay (on average) home to their families. War widows and orphans certainly needed town assistance, though, and the town also helped care for disabled soldiers upon their return, although wounded veterans did receive some federal benefits. The financial outlay for all the towns in New Hampshire was enormous, about $9 million for war expenses. By war's end, Goffstown was nearly $50,000 in debt, a staggering sum in those days. It would take the town until 1878 to pay it off, even though the state assumed $10,000 of it in 1871, which it added to its own monumental debt of $4.5 million.

The war years also saw a tremendous amount of political turmoil in New Hampshire, particularly in Goffstown. In the decades before the Civil War, New Hampshire had been a solidly Democratic state, led by party stalwart

Franklin Pierce, who had served as president of the United States in the 1850s and was New Hampshire's most famous native son. All other political parties—the Whigs, the Free-Soilers, the Know-Nothings—had been decidedly in the minority. The years immediately preceding the outbreak of the war, though, had witnessed the most dramatic political realignment in U.S. history, one that was as apparent in New Hampshire as anywhere else in the North.

Nationally, as the 1850s drew to a close, the Democrats struggled to keep their party together when sectional issues like slavery threatened to tear them apart. Their old political foes the Whigs had already collapsed as a party organization in the 1840s, eventually giving rise to a new party that melded together a broad array of political splinter groups left over from the demise of the Whigs. This new national organization, the Republican Party, embraced a wide variety of reforms, most notably the containment of slavery, although there was a substantial and vocal component within the party that advocated the elimination of slavery altogether. The Republicans had several potential contenders for their party's presidential nomination in 1860, but in the late winter of that year, the young lawyer from Illinois, Abraham Lincoln, began to pull away from the pack, in part because of the reception he had received while on a short speaking tour of New Hampshire in early March when he lectured in both Concord and Manchester. Lincoln's eloquence sparked a wave of Republican sentiment in the state, particularly when the national Democratic Party finally split over the slavery issue. New Hampshire overwhelmingly voted for Lincoln in the presidential election that fall, and his victory led to the South's secession and the outbreak of civil war.

Statewide, New Hampshire Democrats found themselves in the minority once the war started, but not by much. In some other Northern states, the Democratic Party had been all but dismantled, but in New Hampshire it remained a force to be reckoned with, even if the Republicans were in the ascendant. Although Republicans would win the key positions in state government for the next twenty-five years, the Democrats usually made it a close race and were ready to make political capital out of any Republican missteps. During the Civil War, the fortunes of the Republican Party in New Hampshire were very much tied to the progress of the conflict. If Union forces appeared to be gaining the upper hand on the battlefield, Republican sentiment grew stronger among the electorate. Again, this trend was true more or less throughout the North, but it was more pronounced in New Hampshire, where the Democrats remained a potent political organization.

By 1864, relations between the two party organizations in New Hampshire were at their lowest point, a state of affairs that had a dramatic impact on the populace. Most people, even if they did not play an active role in politics, identified strongly with one party over another and displayed their party affiliation for all to see. Political issues were viewed as matters to be openly discussed and debated, and the idea that someone would want to keep his political opinions to himself would have been considered strange indeed. Voter turnout tended to be very high, and voting was considered a public duty not to be shirked. Under these conditions, political disputes easily erupted between those who disagreed.

With the approach of the March 1864 elections, in which New Hampshire citizens would chose their town and state officers, the stakes seemed to be particularly high. The rest of the country had long looked to New Hampshire as a political bellwether because many people believed that these March elections, held so much earlier than in other states, would give some indication as to how the two parties would fare in local elections in other states and how the country as a whole might vote in the coming fall presidential election. New Hampshire residents were keenly conscious of their influence on national politics and therefore imbued their elections with a great deal of importance. The war itself was also at a critical stage. Although the Union forces finally seemed to be beating the Confederates on the battlefield, casualties continued to be very high, and many in the North had had enough of fighting, arguing that it was the right time to negotiate some sort of ceasefire with the South. A portion of the Democratic Party known as Copperheads most vigorously championed this view, even in the early days of the war. Many Democrats did not agree with them, but the Republicans tended to paint all Democrats with the same brush. Republicans took the opposite view—that the war must be prosecuted until the bitter end, no matter the cost. Some Democrats shared this view, too, but they insisted on representing all Republicans as abolitionists who felt little compunction about the deaths of so many soldiers if it brought an end to slavery. Thus the two sides were implacable foes. In January and February, rumors circulated among each party that the other was determined to subvert the democratic process and take over the government by force, which added to the atmosphere of fear and even panic that had begun to pervade politics in the state.

In Goffstown, these fears erupted into a full-fledged fight between Democrats and Republicans on election day, March 8. The details of what actually happened are unknown, but initial newspaper accounts circulated shortly after election night suggested a mighty battle in Goffstown between members of the two parties that had left at least one hundred people dead and many more wounded. In the days that followed, these reports were proven grossly exaggerated, but because the newspapers themselves openly supported one party or the other, it is difficult to piece together a plausible picture of what really happened.

The Republican Manchester newspaper the *Daily Mirror & American* reported the day after the election that the town meeting in Goffstown had been disrupted when a group of Copperhead Democrats had tried to take over using pistols and knives, although the Republicans had been able to elect a moderator before the meeting disintegrated into a fracas. Two days later, the same paper provided a fuller report, stating that the Copperheads had unjustly complained that their rights had been violated and seized the moment to surround the ballot box and take control of the meeting. When a Republican constable had tried to push through the crowd to intervene, he had been knocked over the head. The crowd continued to argue for the rest of the day, and finally the selectmen adjourned the town meeting until the next morning. By that time, the Republicans had contacted the state militia in Manchester, which turned out to maintain order during the following day's balloting, resulting in a clear and resounding Republican victory in the town.

The Democratic Concord newspaper the *New Hampshire Patriot and Gazette* painted a different picture under the headline "War in Goffstown" when it published an account on March 16, more than one week after the election. That paper contended that the Goffstown Republicans had overreacted to a legitimate concern about the townsmen's voting privileges and had tried to intimidate the Democrats with threats of violence and retribution, while the noble Democrats stood firmly in defense of their rights.

Both newspapers cite a third paper called the *Union*, of which apparently no copies survive. It was a Democratic paper from Manchester that painted an even more damaging portrayal of the Republicans' attempt to subvert American democracy, blaming it all on the "Abolitionist Selectmen." But the paper also admitted that no one resorted to violence; rather, the town meeting had become a standoff, with "two hundred good Democrats…[standing] before the ballot-box and [demanding] their *rights*." The state militia, the paper contended, had already been prepared to turn out against the honest citizenry in Manchester if the Democrats caused any trouble there; thus they appeared on the scene at the Goffstown meetinghouse the next day ready to shoot some Copperheads. Alas, Goffstown Democrats were so disgusted by the whole chain of events that they stayed home on the second day, thus allowing the Republicans to claim victory in the election by default.

The truth is probably some mixture of all these accounts, but all the sources seem to agree on a few points. First, despite the rumors of violence, very little fighting actually occurred, although certainly the situation was tense and had the potential to erupt into violence at any moment. The state militia was posted to town on the second day of voting to maintain order. Second, each side claimed that the dispute in Goffstown was proof of a larger conspiracy to deprive the members of their party of their constitutional rights. And third, the stories about the disruption of the Goffstown town meeting traveled far and wide in New Hampshire, substantiating the idea that New Hampshire politics were very divisive indeed in 1864.

In the end, New Hampshire remained a Republican state and would be so for the next several decades. Lincoln won New Hampshire by a comfortable margin in the fall presidential election. The relationship between the state's political parties continued to be tense, but it never reached the low point it had in 1864. By the following year, with the country turning its attention to reconstructing the Union and assimilating the defeated South, even New Hampshire politicians began to get along with one another—or at least they were no longer trying to beat one another up.

GOFFSTOWN'S INDUSTRIAL AGE

Just as the years after the American Revolution had been a period of expansion, innovation and industrialization, so too were the years after the Civil War, as America emerged as an economic force with tremendous potential. In the decades after the war, the United States was transformed from a largely rural, agricultural society into an urban, mechanized one. Even in relatively small towns like Goffstown, this transformation was apparent.

One of the primary requirements of an industrialized economy was a transportation network. New Hampshire's railroads had started in 1838 with a line run to Nashua from Massachusetts. In just four short years, that line had been extended all the way to Concord, setting the stage for the development of the Merrimack Valley that would occur after the war. The line to Concord had been built by the New Hampshire Central Railroad, one of several rail companies in the state that sprang up in the 1830s and 1840s. Initially, the track was planned to run along the west bank of the Merrimack River through Goffstown and the bustling industrial village at Amoskeag. The Amoskeag Manufacturing Company, though, exercised its political might to get the track rerouted to the east bank, where the company was undergoing a major expansion effort. Thus Samuel Blodget's Canal, which had made shipping to Concord feasible in the early part of the nineteenth century, was made irrelevant, and Goffstown was temporarily bypassed by the railroad.

This covered railroad bridge spanned the Piscataquog River in the West Village. *Courtesy of the Goffstown Historical Society, Gerry Hart-Moss Collection.*

The State of New Hampshire was originally rather discouraging to railroad companies and exercised tight control on their activities, thereby limiting their growth. The issue became a major one in state politics, with two Democratic factions battling each other for dominance of the state government in the 1840s. In 1844, one faction emerged victorious and enacted a law that cleared the way for wholesale railroad expansion, placing few restrictions on these corporations. The result was an explosion of new rail lines in the state, as railroad companies tried to establish a vast network of interconnected lines.

Goffstown was part of that expansion, as evidenced by the New Hampshire Central Railroad's construction of a branch line through the center of the town in February 1850. It was part of a line connecting Manchester to Henniker, and ultimately Claremont, although the Henniker–Claremont portion was never built. The track was laid on the south side of the Piscataquog River, running roughly along Mast Road. There were four depots in town, at Goffstown Center (Grasmere), Shirley Station (where Wallace Road intersects Mast Road), Goffstown Village and Parker's Village (near the New Boston line), which from this point forward was referred to as Parker Station. Eventually, other railroads built branch lines through the town—one from Parker Station to New Boston (1893–1935) and another from Goffstown Center to Bedford, Amherst and Milford (built in 1899). The town's various lines passed through several owners before being bought by the Boston & Maine Railroad in 1895.

The West Village depot became the primary railroad stop in Goffstown. *Courtesy of the Goffstown Historical Society, Gerry Hart-Moss Collection.*

The Boston & Maine had risen to prominence in New Hampshire in the second half of the nineteenth century, and shortly after 1900, it was the only railroad in the state, controlling all but fifty miles of New Hampshire's track. Rail service became vital to the development of Goffstown, underlying all the economic changes—agricultural and industrial—that were to come.

The Amoskeag Manufacturing Company that had inspired industry along the Merrimack in the 1820s also encouraged other manufacturers to build mills in Goffstown along the Piscataquog River. Gristmills and sawmills had been in use along the river dating back to the town's settlement, but by the 1850s these mills were increasingly being converted to factories that produced a wide array of products—pails, matches, furniture, boxes, textiles, mattresses, hosiery, windows, sashes, blinds, doors, carriages, sleds, needles, stoves, paint, varnishes, plumbing supplies, hats, shoes and cigars. All were produced in Goffstown in the nineteenth and early twentieth centuries on a greater or lesser scale, with companies forming and folding on a regular basis. The most substantial manufactories included a paper and pulp mill in Goffstown Center, a huge facility with an enormous tower that rose high into the sky. Although it had several owners over the years (including Goffstown resident and governor of New Hampshire P.C. Cheney) and burned down repeatedly, it remained in operation throughout the second half of the nineteenth century before the owners decided to close up shop in 1910 after

P.C. Cheney's Paper and Pulp Mill in Grasmere on the Piscataquog River. *Courtesy of the Goffstown Historical Society, Gerry Hart-Moss Collection.*

yet another fire. Another large factory was the bobbin shop, which also went through numerous owners during its several decades of existence, although it is best known by the name of its last owners, the Hambleton brothers. Under their direction in the early part of the twentieth century, the mill became the largest bobbin and spool factory in New England.

By far the town's most important industry, though, was the Kendall-Hadley Sash and Blind Company. Founded in 1868 by Kendrick Kendall, Henry W. Hadley and Lewis H. Stark, it was a steam-powered factory located in the West Village, constructed on what had been one of the town's militia muster fields. The company enjoyed tremendous success during its more than one hundred years in operation. In 1870, just two years after it opened, it employed forty people (five of them children) and produced fifty thousand sashes and twenty-five thousand blinds annually, more than any of the town's three other sash and blind companies. At its peak in the early twentieth century, it employed about seventy-five men. Although it, too, passed through different owners over the years, it made some of the finest window sashes and blinds in New England, supplying contractors as far away as Boston and New York City. The factory remained in operation until 1982.

The nature of agriculture changed again and dramatically during these years as well. The sheep craze of the first half of the nineteenth century

The Kendall-Hadley Sash and Blind Company, which was torn down in the 1980s. *Courtesy of the Goffstown Historical Society, Snay Collection.*

had a brief resurgence during the Civil War, particularly as Southern cotton was no longer available. But by 1870, the demand for New England wool had subsided for good. In that year, Goffstown farmers owned only about one-third of the number of sheep they had in 1850 and produced less than one-fifth of the amount of wool, just over six hundred pounds. Midwestern sheep farms, which produced wool in far larger quantities, supplanted New England farms, with the railroads bringing in the midwestern wool at cheap prices. The railroad also brought an end to the days of New England grain and grass production, as midwestern farms produced larger quantities at cheaper prices, all shipped to the East by train.

Instead, New England farmers concentrated on supplying perishable foodstuffs, which could not be shipped from the Midwest. New England became a land of dairy farmers, providing milk, eggs, cheese and butter to large eastern cities like Boston, Portsmouth and Portland. Vermont, which had had many more sheep than New Hampshire, took the lead in this switch to dairy, becoming internationally known for its dairy products long before the advent of Ben & Jerry's ice cream. But New Hampshire shared in these new products as well, albeit on a smaller scale. New England farmers also promoted the sale of fruits and vegetables in greater quantities than ever before, as well as more traditional homegrown products like maple syrup, jams, jellies and ice (which was a major industry in northern New England until the 1950s and the introduction of electric refrigerators in homes). All of these goods were transported by rail, many of them packed into freight cars loaded with ice, allowing them to arrive at their destinations relatively fresh, something the Midwest could not do at this time.

Despite all these changes, New England farms suffered in the second half of the nineteenth century. In larger numbers than ever before, people started abandoning their farms and moving elsewhere—to industrial jobs in the city or to new opportunities in the West. In 1850, there had been almost 275 farms in town. Ten years later, that number dropped to just under 200, and another ten years after that, it had dropped again to just over 150. Several groups formed to provide support for farmers, including, on the national level, the Grange (also called the Patrons of Husbandry) and, more locally, the Piscataquog Valley Association. Both hosted lectures about agriculture, organized social events and sponsored agricultural fairs at Goffstown's fairgrounds located near Shirley Station. Although these types

A popular series of maps depicted a bird's-eye panorama view of many towns in the late 1800s. This one of Goffstown was made in 1877. *Courtesy of the Library of Congress.*

of organizations gave farmers a stronger support network and made farming a more attractive way of life, they could not reverse the general downward trend of agriculture during this period. The other attack on agriculture in the late nineteenth century was cultural. Life in a rural community with its traditional ways no longer seemed appealing to many people, and the country in general began to perceive farmers as backward and too set in their ways. America was entering the modern era, with big cities, factories, public transportation systems, entertainment, stores and restaurants, and young people didn't want to be left behind on the farm.

As a predominantly rural state, New Hampshire as a whole lost residents during this period. In 1860, the population of New Hampshire actually declined by 2 percent, even though in the rest of the United States it grew substantially, with some sources estimating the national average growth rate at 25 percent or more. Goffstown's population fell in these years as well. In the 1870s, the state's population recovered, fueled mainly by the immigration of large numbers of people from Canada, many of whom were abandoning farms for the more stable factory work offered by U.S. manufacturing. By the end of the century, these population shifts had produced some dramatic and unforeseen results in New Hampshire, and in Goffstown, that would change the town's structure and challenge the townspeople's traditional Yankee culture.

THE WAR OF THE
TOWN HALLS

O ne result of the massive industrialization of the mid-nineteenth century was the rise of the West Village as Goffstown's primary commercial center. With the nearby falls providing a potential source of power and a ford in the river for Mast Road, the West Village had had some settlements since the early 1800s. As more factories were constructed near this part of the river in mid-century, however, more and more people set up businesses and moved to the West Village, including the town's Congregational church, several stores and the New Hampshire Central Hotel. The West Village also served as the crossroads for several important roadways linking the town to New Boston, Weare and Dunbarton. Goffstown's West Village was the most substantial commercial center of all three towns and thus drew business from them. In addition, the West Village's train depot was located right in the middle of town, whereas the depot for Goffstown Center (Grasmere) was located on the other side of the river from most residences. By the time of the Civil War, the West Village had definitively become the economic and social center of the town, while Goffstown Center had remained a somewhat sleepy country village.

As a result of all the growth that Goffstown had sustained in the mid-nineteenth century, many of the townspeople thought the town had outgrown the old meetinghouse—its size, its colonial character and its location. In 1869, the town voted to sell the meetinghouse to some private investors,

Grasmere near the end of the nineteenth century. *Courtesy of the Goffstown Historical Society, Snay Collection.*

who moved it to the corner of Elm and Auburn Streets in Manchester, where several years later it burned down. The money from the sale went to construct a new town hall in the West Village at a cost of roughly $5,000, which included such modern conveniences as heat—a luxury that had been lacking in the old meetinghouse.

Twenty years later, town residents wanted to expand and renovate the new town hall, but it was here that they hit a snag. The people who lived in Goffstown Center deeply resented the decline of their village's prestige within the township, which was symbolized by the loss of the old meetinghouse. At the town meeting of 1889, during which residents would vote on appropriating the money for the town hall renovation, a group of people from Goffstown Center issued their fellow townsmen an ultimatum: unless the town voted the funds to build another town hall in Goffstown Center, they would make sure the appropriation for the town hall in the West Village was voted down. Remarkably, the people of the West Village agreed and literally shook hands to seal the bargain. The town of Goffstown suddenly found itself in possession of not one town hall but two.

At almost the same time as the town voted to build a second town hall, Goffstown Center was given a new name—Grasmere. Its origin was English,

Grasmere Town Hall. *Courtesy of the Goffstown Historical Society, Gerry Hart-Moss Collection.*

specifically an English village in the Lake District that was home to some poets known as the Lake Poets (including William Wordsworth, who described Grasmere, England, as "the loveliest spot that man hath ever found"). Substituting the name of Grasmere for Goffstown Center was proposed by P.C. Cheney, the former governor of New Hampshire and owner of the paper and pulp mill on the Piscataquog, who had relatives in Grasmere, England. Thus, the new town hall would be called the Grasmere Town Hall, although technically there was no town of Grasmere and the building was not built to serve as a true town hall.

Designed by noted Manchester architect William W. Ireland, the Grasmere Town Hall was constructed in a matter of months in 1889 for $4,500 on the same location where the old meetinghouse had stood. Built in the Queen Anne style so popular at the time, it proved a thoroughly useful building over the years, housing Grasmere Schoolhouse No. 9 (both primary and grammar schools), a district court and a dinner theatre and serving as a meeting place for all kinds of government and community groups, including the Junior Grange, the Order of United Mechanics, the Knights of Pythias and later the Goffstown Garden Club, the Knights of Columbus, the Grasmere Water Precinct, the Goffstown Historic District Commission, Goffstown Junior Baseball, Tri-Town Soccer and the Friends of the Rail Trail, among many others. The building was listed on the National Register of Historic Places

Town Hall, Goffstown, N. H.

This page and opposite:: The Opera House in the Village. To the horror of townspeople, it burned down on March 11, 1937. *Courtesy of the Goffstown Historical Society, Gerry Hart-Moss Collection.*

in 1990 and has undergone a substantial renovation in the late twentieth and early twenty-first centuries, the first in its history.

The fate of the town hall, located in the West Village (which became known simply as the Village from this point on), proved far different. After the town vote approved funds for its renovation in 1889, it was substantially enlarged and modified at a cost of $6,500, more than the building had initially cost to construct just twenty years before. The new structure, though, was the town's pride and joy. Also constructed in the Queen Anne style, it boasted a majestic turret (which saw the addition of a clock in 1890) and grand meeting spaces on its two floors that served as the home for countless community celebrations in the coming years. From the date of its renovation in 1889, it was known as the Opera House, although no professional operas were ever performed there. The building not only served as the seat of government for the town but also as its social center, hosting plays, performances, dinners and all sorts of ceremonies. Its destruction by fire in 1937 was considered a devastating loss by the townspeople. All that remains of this once impressive building is a small round portion that was placed on a lot off Church Street and became known as the Little Round House.

BAPTISM BY FIRE

On the night of February 18, 1892, a fire raced through the nearly finished building that was to house the new Benedictine school, Saint Anselm College. Beginning at about eight o'clock, the flames had become visible to people in Manchester by 10:00 p.m., but fire crews had trouble reaching the inferno, slowed by deep snow that bogged down their equipment. When they did arrive on the scene, they discovered that there was no water with which to fight the blaze. By the time it burned itself out, the fire had consumed nearly the entire structure, representing almost a complete loss for the college.

The fire marked an inauspicious beginning for what was touted as only the third Catholic college in New England (following Boston College and the College of the Holy Cross). It was to be neither the first nor the last hurdle in establishing this new institution. In fact, the first years of the college's history were characterized by trials and travails that might have overwhelmed less determined men. But Saint Anselm College, like Goffstown itself, would strive to reinvent itself time and again in its effort to survive the changing times. The fire simply marked the first of its many rebirths.

The inspiration behind the idea of creating a Catholic college in New Hampshire belonged to the first head of the Manchester diocese, Bishop Denis Bradley, who came to Manchester in April 1884 when the diocese was created. Bradley was a man of vision who welcomed the challenges of ministering to Manchester's large and primarily foreign Catholic population. Most of the Catholics in Manchester were of Irish or French-Canadian

The shell of Saint Anselm College was all that remained after the devastating fire of February 18, 1892. *Courtesy of Saint Anselm College Archives, Geisel Library, Saint Anselm College, Manchester, New Hampshire.*

descent, but in the 1870s, the Amoskeag Manufacturing Company began hiring more and more German immigrants, many of whom were Catholic. In 1887, worried that the Germans would drift away from the faith unless supported by a ministry that could preach to them in their own language, Bishop Bradley asked the Benedictine order of St. Mary's headquartered in New Jersey to send a priest for this German contingent of his flock, as these Benedictines were primarily of German extraction themselves. Bradley also suggested that the Benedictines found a college in Manchester, believing that it would promote Catholicism in general in New Hampshire. In response, St. Mary's Abbot Hilary Pfraengle sent Father Sylvester Joerg with orders to pursue both of Bradley's charges and with promises of financial support from St. Mary's. The first part of Joerg's assignment was completed with relatively little fuss. Within a year, he had established St. Raphael's Church on the west side of Manchester, which became the spiritual and social center of the German community there.

The second part of Joerg's assignment was not so easily accomplished. With Bradley's help, Abbot Hilary and Joerg quickly found an appropriate site on which to locate the college, a rural hillside overlooking the city of Manchester with plenty of room for the college's future expansion. It was here, though, that the college encountered its first setback. With nearly all of Manchester's working-class population coming from a Catholic background, the city of

Manchester itself did not suffer from much anti-Catholic sentiment. The workers were too numerous and too important to the functioning of the enormous mill complex on which everyone's welfare was based. Outside of Manchester, though, it was a different story. Since all of its residents professed some form of Protestantism, Goffstown had not experienced any significant religious strife for one hundred years. There might have been denominational and cultural differences, but people in Goffstown had more or less learned to live with one another, eventually assimilating to such an extent that they were all Protestant New Englanders who essentially shared the same values and Anglo-American background. The thousands of Catholic immigrants who had been coming to Manchester since the 1840s only served to reinforce this idea, emphasizing the difference between Goffstown's Yankee citizens and the foreigners who were coming to America in unprecedented numbers. This view was in fact prevalent throughout much of the United States at the time, as the late nineteenth century witnessed the arrival of foreign immigrants on a scale never before imagined. Catholicism became a defining feature of this foreignness, and many native-born Americans viewed Catholics with deep distrust and suspicion.

This anti-Catholic bias became apparent when Joerg went to establish the new college. Fearing that the Yankee farmers would refuse to sell land to Catholics, the Benedictines relied on the help of local supporters who did not have noticeably foreign or Catholic names to facilitate purchases of land. In 1891, the Benedictines purchased a collection of farms in the southeastern corner of Goffstown, beginning with the Kimball farm, a parcel of about eighty acres. Other properties surrounding the Kimball farm were added over the years until the college reached its present size of roughly four hundred acres.

The name chosen for the new school was Saint Anselm, after the eleventh-century English archbishop of Canterbury who was also famous as a great scholastic theologian. The name was actually the Benedictines' second choice. They had originally wanted to call the school Saint Bede, but another Catholic college forming in Illinois claimed the name before them. So Saint Anselm it was. Their choice was motivated in part by an attempt to appease anti-Catholic feeling in the surrounding community. After all, Anselm of Canterbury had been English, just as had the ancestors of many of the residents of Goffstown and the other towns in the Merrimack Valley.

Later that same year, construction began on the college's only building, which would house the monks and students while also providing office and classroom space. The neighbors were either not as anti-Catholic as

Hilary had feared or they came around quickly to the idea of having a Catholic college nearby, because some of them helped with the excavation work for the new building. Most of the construction, though, was done by a Manchester firm, the Head and Dowst Company. All but the finishing touches had been completed when the fire occurred on February 18, 1892. Officially, no cause has ever been established, and rumors circulated for years afterward that the fire had been deliberately set by townspeople who could not abide the idea of a conclave of Catholics in their midst. More likely, though, is the theory that a boiler located in the basement of the building had been incorrectly tapped down for the night, thus sparking the conflagration. Either way, it was a complete disaster for the college, which was already struggling for funds.

Rather than abandoning the project, though, reconstruction began just two weeks after the fire but with a slightly modified design. The financial fallout from the fire was complicated by the fact that technically the contractor was responsible for all the damage, as the building was still under the company's control at the time of the disaster. In an effort to speed reconstruction efforts and avoid lengthy lawsuits, the Benedictines assumed some of the debt from the construction company, even though it placed them in an even more precarious financial position.

The new college building was completed in the late summer of the following year. When finished, it rose five stories high and included New Hampshire granite that had been dug out of a rock shelf that lay right in front of the building. The college admitted its first students the following month, on September 6, 1893. For the next ten or more years, the college barely survived, as its enrollment fluctuated greatly before eventually settling at about one hundred students. Teaching these students was a faculty of fifteen, composed almost entirely of priests or those studying for the priesthood. For the students, attending a Catholic college in America at this time was a demanding venture. Students were held to a very strict code of conduct that bore more similarities to monastic life than the college experience most people think of today. For example, thirteen members of the college's renowned baseball team were expelled from the college when they returned late from an away game even though they were accompanied by their coach. This rather draconian punishment had a negative effect on enrollment in the late 1890s.

The course of study was very different from modern colleges as well. In fact, Saint Anselm College was originally more of a preparatory boys' school than an institution of higher learning. Most of the students took classes that

A highly idealized early twentieth-century postcard depiction of Saint Anselm College and the surrounding community. *Courtesy of the Goffstown Historical Society, Grant Collection.*

prepared them for college. There were even a few very young boys who were in a seventh- and eighth-grade program called a minim. Once students completed these preparatory courses, they could move on to the college's higher education program, which consisted of three tracks. The commercial track was a three-year course of study geared toward students who hoped to enter professional fields (mainly business) after graduation. The classical track was a five-year course of study that followed the lines of a more traditional liberal arts education, which was heavily based on philosophy and the classics. The theological track was also a five-year course of study and was designed for those hoping to enter the priesthood.

As tuition was quite high, most of the students came not from the surrounding area but from some of the wealthier Catholic families from the Northeast. Yet despite the sums paid by the student body, the college limped along financially in its early years. Abbot Hilary, who took the unprecedented step of running the college himself for five years (which meant he had to take a leave of absence from his duties at St. Mary's), embarked on an ambitious program of fundraising to supplement student fees. The most successful efforts included subscription Masses (when donors essentially bought Masses for themselves or loved ones for a substantial fee) and the practice of loaning out money to area Catholics at a moderate rate of interest, which became successful when large numbers of Catholic workers proved suspicious of

This unusual photo of Saint Anselm College in the 1890s emphasizes the college's rural setting. The monks' vineyards can be seen in the foreground. *Courtesy of Saint Anselm College Archives, Geisel Library, Saint Anselm College, Manchester, New Hampshire.*

regular banks. Abbot Hilary also worked relentlessly to garner more financial support from the Manchester diocese, knowing that the brotherhood at St. Mary's was already contributing everything it could to the college. The diocese seemed reluctant to support the college in this way, at least at the level Abbot Hilary felt necessary. But when faced with the possibility of the college closing or the Benedictines turning it over to a different religious order, the Manchester diocese increased its financial support as well.

The college also strove to be economically diverse during this early period, and for many years, it remained a working farm. On its grounds, the Benedictines maintained a bakery; raised livestock such as horses, cattle, pigs and chickens; managed an orchard, garden and vineyards; and had a beekeeper who produced substantial quantities of honey. These products brought in additional revenue for the college and helped it become more self-sufficient. This diversification also brought the members of the college into greater contact with the townspeople, as they sold some of their products locally and often hired townspeople as manual laborers during busy periods.

Transformations of a New England Town

By 1905, when Abbot Hilary returned to St. Mary's in New Jersey, the college had finally achieved some stability with steady enrollments and a slowly improving financial future. By 1911, it was economically stable enough to pay off some of its more onerous debts and build an addition to the school. America's entry into World War I in 1917 presented another challenge for the school, both because of the loss of students to the war effort and because of the college's historically German roots. The Benedictines made a concerted effort to emphasize their American character and downplay the German background of many of their brothers, and it seemed to work. Although nearby Pinardville had at least one episode of a German family being hounded out of the neighborhood, no such events occurred at the college.

Whatever losses the college suffered during the war were compensated for in the postwar boom. In fact, the college's finances were so strong that it started its own abbey in 1927, finally severing the connection with St. Mary's in New Jersey. At the same time, the preparatory course of study was gradually phased out during these first decades of the twentieth century until it was discontinued altogether in 1935. World War II proved another defining moment for the college, as it began functioning more as a modern college and less as a monastic enclave. By the end of the war, the percentage of faculty who were not priests had risen dramatically, and the curriculum had been redesigned to more closely resemble that of other colleges. Many of the strict rules governing students' behavior were also dropped or significantly scaled back. In 1958, the college created a lay board, which ushered in a period of dramatically increased enrollment and a building boom that formed the basis of the modern campus. By the middle of the twentieth century, Saint Anselm College had become both the largest employer and the biggest taxpayer in Goffstown, yet the college somehow remained almost segregated from the town itself, having very little interaction with town affairs. If Goffstown residents had worried that the introduction of a Catholic college would alter their traditional New England township, they were proved wrong.

THE FIRST OLD HOME
CELEBRATION

The number of immigrants moving to the Merrimack Valley was not the only reason Goffstown residents feared that their Yankee culture was under siege in the late nineteenth century. The very idea of traditional New England seemed on the brink of extinction, as country villages all over the region fell into a steep decline. Determined to halt this decay, New England towns embarked on an ambitious program to reinvigorate their rural communities with the newly developed Old Home celebrations at their center.

In the years after the Civil War, people started leaving New Hampshire in unprecedented numbers, particularly the small townships located far from urban centers that had dotted the landscape since colonial days. Tired of struggling on unproductive New England farms in extreme weather conditions, many young people moved to the cities to take on industrial or service jobs. Others tried their hands at farming in the West, where land was cheap, plentiful and fertile. New Hampshire suddenly became a popular place to hail *from*, with Sons of New Hampshire societies springing up all over the country, even in such distant cities as Chicago and San Francisco. Many towns in New Hampshire saw their populations plummet to less than half of what they had been in the first half of the century. Some of them would never recover those pre-war population levels again.

Although Goffstown shared this rural character with many other New Hampshire towns, it was insulated from an extreme loss because of its proximity to Manchester, where opportunities were more plentiful than in the country. The town did lose residents after 1860, with the population of 1870 standing at just over two-thirds of what it had been in 1850, but the decline was not as steep as in other towns. By 1900, it had rebounded and was at its highest level in the town's history, possibly because of the introduction of the electric railway that linked it to Manchester, where the arrival of more and more workers bolstered the population.

In the first decade of the twentieth century, Goffstown would see its own massive influx of immigrants in both the French-Canadian development of Pinardville and the arrival of large groups of Greek and Turkish immigrants to work in the Hambleton brothers' Bobbin Shop. The Greeks outnumbered the Turks and settled along the banks of the Piscataquog River within walking distance of the factory in which they labored. The townspeople could not help but notice these unique and distinct ethnic groups within their midst, particularly as the two groups bore a centuries-old grudge against each other, brought over from the southern European countries whence they came. In fact, sometime about 1905, the tension between these two ethnic groups erupted in a riot near Depot Street, where the Greek community was based. All of these factors combined to make native New Englanders feel that their town—and their way of life—were threatened by a cultural demise.

To counter the declining population and perceived cultural dissolution, towns across New Hampshire took steps to promote their traditional Yankee heritage, such as publishing their town histories (which usually had a heavy focus on the colonial period) and erecting monuments to what they considered their town's most worthy citizens (often Revolutionary or Civil War soldiers, along with famous native sons). Goffstown was rather late to adopt both of these measures, with the town's history not being published until 1922 (a 1,200-page tome written by George P. Hadley) and the town's first—and to date only—statue (a Civil War soldier) being erected in 1916.

Goffstown did, however, embrace another measure to celebrate the town's heritage, one that towns across New Hampshire were also instituting: the introduction of an Old Home celebration. The idea was a simple one—encourage local communities to spruce themselves up and throw a giant festival celebrating everything about them. Hopefully, former residents would return to visit family and friends and see how glorious life in their old towns could be. Old Home celebrations were the brainchild of New Hampshire's governor, Frank Rollins, a banker, politician and promoter who claimed descent from one of New Hampshire's earliest families. Although Rollins had extensive business dealings in Boston and New York, he had chosen to keep his home in New Hampshire, where he touted the benefits of rural country life. In 1899, he began promoting the idea of Old Home celebrations and thereby "kindling the fires of state patriotism," as he put it. Rollins was not against the immigrant influx into the state; rather, he claimed he wanted to show those immigrants what it meant to be Americans. Old Home celebrations, he asserted, offered a way to speed immigrant assimilation into American culture. The state formed an Old Home Week Association and compiled a packet of information for town committees to help them organize their community events.

Initially, the festivals were intended to last one week and feature a wide variety of activities that would show off towns to their best advantage, including parades, banquets, speeches, church services, baseball games, firemen musters, dances and historical pageants. Townspeople spent months preparing their communities, painting, repairing roads and bridges, building new schools, renovating town buildings and so on. To emphasize the connection between New Hampshire towns, each town was supposed to light a bonfire on its highest hill on a particular night so that people would be able to see the fires of all the communities around them and thus feel their ties to the state strengthened. To coordinate these

"THE UNCANOONUCS"

The Town of Goffstown

through its "Old Home Week Association" cordially invites her absent sons and daughters, and all former residents to come back once more and mingle in the festivities incident to

"Old Home Day"

on THURSDAY, SEPTEMBER 1, 1904. Exercises befitting the occasion will be observed, while on the Sunday previous, services on the "Old Home" theme will be conducted in the churches.

Let all return to this reunion and review the scenes and incidents of earlier years, so pleasant and truly profitable to recall.

WM. H. STINSON,
Secretary.

GEORGE P. HADLEY,
President.
Old Home Week Association.

Goffstown, N. H., 1904   **"BE WISE AND COME"**

Organizers sent this postcard as a reminder for the town's upcoming first Old Home celebrations to be held on September 1, 1904. *Courtesy of the Goffstown Historical Society, Gerry Hart-Moss Collection.*

A Poem Written for the First Old Home Celebration
By Moses Gage Shirley
September 1, 1904

An Excerpt

Back to the Goffstown hills today
    We give you hearty greeting,
For Old Home Week we celebrate
    When old-time friends we're meeting.

Back to the Uncanoonucs, twain,
    Whose crests are reared to heaven,
Where the first beams of morning rest,
    And the last glow of even.

Back to the swift Piscataquog,
    Our bright and bonnie river,
Which like the stream in poet's song
    Is flowing on forever.

Back to the scenes of long ago
    And childhood's happy dreaming,
To lay aside dull care and grief,
    And worldly ways and scheming.

Back to the valleys and the hills
    Today we gladly greet you;
And whether Joe or whether Bill,
    We say we're glad to meet you.

Renew the ties of other days
    In fair and cloudy weather;
Clasp hands again and all rejoice,
    Once more we are together. . . .

Goffstown is glad to welcome back
    All who from her have tarried,
And elsewhere may have cast their lot
    And settled down and married.

We welcome all to breathe once more
    The pure air of the mountains,
And drink from crystal springs as clear
    As any old-world fountains.

Come back and wander o'er the hills
    And by each hallowed spot,
Which with you ever will abide
    And cannot be forgot.

The village green, the stately trees
    O'er-arching many a street,
The church-spires pointing to the sky,
    Where is the sight more sweet?

We bid you welcome with the hope
    That when you shall depart
Fond memories of the homeland still
    Will cluster round each heart,

Till the last scenes of earth shall fade
    Upon some fairer shore.
It will be Old Home Week in Heavan
    And we shall part no more.

This poem was written by Moses Gage Shirley, the town's resident poet, in honor of the first Old Home Celebration.

activities, all towns had to hold their festivals at roughly the same time, around September 1.

The first few communities held their Old Home Week fairs in 1901, but Goffstown did not organize its own until 1904. Organizers sent out 1,100 invitations to "the many absent sons and daughters and former residents," as a pamphlet commemorating the event states. The big day itself—Thursday, September 1—began with the ringing of bells and the blowing of steam whistles at 7:00 a.m. The town had been decorated with banners and streamers, buildings had been painted and public services repaired in preparation for the crowds. The weather was reportedly beautiful for most of the day, although clouds rolled in late in the afternoon. The program was extensive and included many of the activities that were considered standard fare for such town celebrations: a firemen's muster, a concert by the Goffstown Cornet Band, a tennis tournament, a shooting demonstration by the Goffstown Gun Club, a baseball game between the town's two baseball teams, the reading of a poem written specially for the occasion by Goffstown's resident poet Moses Gage Shirley and a long list of speeches. The Opera House also hosted a dinner for 1,300 people, many of whom had arrived in town by train early that morning. The town's former residents who had returned for the festivities got to eat first, while the current town residents had to take their chances that the food supplies would hold out. The day was deemed a success, and for several years thereafter, Goffstown hosted similar Old Home Week celebrations.

Other towns found Old Home Week equally as beneficial, offering residents a chance to celebrate their town's accomplishments and sometimes even luring former residents back to town again, either as year-round residents or as summer residents drawn by New Hampshire's growing tourist industry. Remarkably, former residents did attend these events in staggering numbers, sometimes traveling great distances to do so. Those who could not attend often wrote congratulatory letters to the town organizers, reminiscing about the time they spent there. Occasionally these former residents even assisted towns financially, giving donations or establishing endowments to support specific town ventures. The construction of many a library or town common in New Hampshire was funded in just such a way. Although there is no record of such donations in Goffstown, the town did embark on an improvement program at roughly this same time. The town built the north common in 1907 at the central intersection in the Village on a spot formerly occupied by two large buildings that had recently burned down. The soldier's monument was erected on this common a few years later. In 1909, the town constructed Memorial Library on the site of what sources claim was "an ancient tavern," which was moved to make way for the new building. The library's collection, donated mostly by resident Lucy Rogers in 1880, had previously resided in the selectmen's room of the Opera House and been available to

This home was one of the earliest constructed in the Village and served for many years as a tavern before it was moved to make way for the new library in 1909. *Courtesy of the Goffstown Historical Society, Snay Collection.*

residents on a very limited basis. The grand design for Memorial Library, constructed in brick, standing at the town's major intersection across from the new common, gave an added sense of solidity to the Village.

The town's civic improvements coincided with a rise in the number of social organizations emerging in the town. Most noteworthy of the many groups that formed during this period to promote various activities and strengthen the town's social network was the Young Ladies Dramatic Club, which routinely staged large productions in the Opera House, from dances to plays to musical recitals. This organization nearly single-handedly kept the community entertained in the early part of the twentieth century. Goffstown was also home to one of the first Boy Scout troops in the United States, formed in town in 1911 as Eagle Troop No. 1. The founders had been inspired by the Boy Scout movement that had started in Great Britain in 1907 and was just starting to make an appearance in the United States. Goffstown's group, which began with thirty-two young men, was active a full five years before the national Boy Scouts of America organization was founded.

All of these activities occurred during the peak years of Old Home Week celebrations in New Hampshire, encouraged by the celebrations' stirring of patriotism and community spirit. Between 1900 and 1917, about 120 New Hampshire towns hosted Old Home Weeks, and the idea spread quickly to the rest of New England as well. Old Home Weeks even began to appear in towns in Canada and the Midwest.

America's entry into World War I refocused most people's attention away from local concerns and toward international ones. These types of community festivals were rarely seen in the 1920s, and most towns stopped holding Old Home Week celebrations. But in the first decade and a half of the twentieth century, Old Home Week proved an important annual event that reinforced community members' bonds with one another, bonds that would soon be put to the test by the arrival of a whole new group of people who would strive to make the town their own.

EDMOND PINARD,
LAND DEVELOPER

The area known today as Pinardville was still largely rural at the turn of the twentieth century, but with Manchester's population growing dramatically every decade, it could not remain so for long. In 1906, a bartender turned merchant named Edmond Pinard conceived the idea of establishing a large settlement of his fellow French-Canadians there, thus introducing a community of immigrants who would challenge Goffstown's Yankee self-image.

Of French-Canadian descent himself, Pinard was born in Quebec in 1857 and immigrated to Manchester when he was just sixteen years old. He worked as a bartender and a grocer, finally becoming the owner of a market near Bridge Street. In 1906, he turned his attention to an area of farmland in southeastern Goffstown and decided to become a land developer. Relatively few people lived in this section of town, which was divided by Mast Road as it headed toward Manchester and the Merrimack River. Moses Kelley's colonial tavern was still there, and Saint Anselm College had been built on a hill overlooking the area in the 1890s. There was also a collection of farms, a few of them quite large, owned by families such as the Libbys and the Bartletts. The other major property holder was the Roy family, which owned large tracts of land on the south side of Mast Road.

Pinard quickly bought up a huge parcel of farmland on the north side of Mast Road, filed development plans with the town to subdivide this land

Edmond Pinard.

into house lots and built a market, which he operated himself for the first few years. In 1909, he sold the market to the Levesque family, another group of French-Canadian émigrés, who turned it into the economic and social center of the community.

Pinard himself concentrated on laying out his new development and bringing in families to live in it. In realizing this ambition, though, he encountered some opposition from the Roy brothers, who—like many others in America at that time—did not look kindly on having their traditional Yankee community swamped by the arrival of a large group of foreigners, particularly as these foreigners were Catholics. Powerless to stop Pinard from developing his property, they nevertheless vowed to maintain a distinction between the New Englanders on one side and the French-Canadians on the other, which is why the streets that branch off from either side of Mast Road do not line up. The northern side was laid out by Pinard while the southern side was laid out by the Roys. Nevertheless, at some point—and quite soon after Pinard began developing his property—the whole region became known as Pinardville.

Whatever might have been his thoughts about the conflict with the Roy brothers, Pinard was undeterred in his efforts. He laid out the streets on his side of town and named some of them after relatives. He marked out lots that were forty by one hundred feet and began to sell them to prospective homeowners. He also donated twelve acres of land for the establishment of a Catholic church, the aptly named St. Edmond's, which became an important focal point for the community after it was constructed in 1911. Naturally, the church provided spiritual guidance for the French-Canadians who moved to the area, but it also opened a school as an alternative to the town schools that were already there, provided assistance for parishioners in need and ran an active program of social events for the community that included dances, plays and all sorts of celebrations. There was no doubt that the area's culture was French-Canadian, just as the Roy brothers had feared. In fact, French, not English, became the predominant language in Pinardville.

The French-Canadians' sense of community was reinforced by their relative sense of isolation from both Manchester and Goffstown. Manchester lay right across the Piscataquog River with only Kelley Falls, named after colonial figure Moses Kelley, separating them. The falls had been dammed in 1890 by the Union Electric Company, but there was no bridge connecting the two banks of the river other than a red covered train bridge that local Pinardville residents dubbed "Le Pont Rouge." Reaching Pinardville from Manchester meant going around the long way, across a small bridge over the Piscataquog that lay near its convergence with the Merrimack. The only other alternative was to go into Grasmere and cross the river there, doubling back toward Pinardville. Residents could travel along Mast Road by foot or horse. Increasingly, they could take an automobile or they could ride the streetcar that extended to the Bartlett brothers' icehouse. This spot was known as the Limit, because it was here that the streetcars stopped. Starting in July 1900, trolleys going all the way to Goffstown Village began service from this point. The streetcar thus provided Pinardville residents with a means to commute to their jobs in the Amoskeag Manufacturing Company in Manchester, where the vast majority of the French-Canadians worked.

It was not until 1914 that a street bridge was erected over Kelley Falls linking Goffstown to Manchester. The strange story of the bridge's construction illustrates the distaste with which the French-Canadians were viewed by the larger community. Pinard promoted the construction of the bridge, no doubt recognizing what it would do for his land development project, and allowed his land to be used on the Pinardville side of the bridge. Construction duly began, but midway through, Manchester residents on the other side of the river put up so many obstacles that its location on the other side had to be shifted. Thus the direction of the bridge had to be altered in mid-construction, resulting in a bridge with an angle. The twenty-degree turn in the Kelley Street Bridge looked very odd indeed, earning it a place in *Ripley's Believe It or Not* at one point. It was also the source of several accidents over the years when motorists misjudged the turn and plunged off the bridge. Several efforts were made to decrease the angle without totally

A postcard of the Kelley Falls Bridge and its famous twenty-degree angle. *Courtesy of Dan LaRochelle.*

rebuilding the bridge, although it wasn't until 1974 that the bridge was torn down and replaced with a new one, which still bears a curve.

The bridge did much to further the development of Pinardville. In the decades that followed the span's construction, Pinardville blossomed and spread far beyond the bounds of Pinard's original holdings. The area remained predominantly French-Canadian and Catholic well into the second half of the twentieth century, which is evident by the names of its streets, businesses and many of its residents. In 1915, there was a serious effort to separate Pinardville from Goffstown and annex it to Manchester, but with a city full of new immigrant arrivals, Manchester was not enthusiastic about adding more and squashed the effort. The episode emphasized Pinardville's separate identity from the rest of the town, though, and illustrated how the French-Canadian residents felt a greater kinship to urban Manchester than to rural Goffstown. There was even a French language newspaper called *La Press* in the area for awhile, another feature that set the French-Canadian community apart. In the 1930s, the Rhode Island Land Company bought up lots in the area and began to promote them aggressively, leading to another settlement boom for Pinardville. Many of these residents were not French-Canadians, and although the area retained some of its French-Canadian characteristics, it began to revert to a more Yankee culture, particularly as the French-Canadians themselves, who were second- or third-generation Americans by this time, began to identify with the larger community rather than the small circle of their parents and grandparents.

SUMMER PEOPLE

Not everyone living in rural New Hampshire saw the declining farm population and the abandoned farms as a bad thing. For some, it represented an opportunity. Yet again, New Hampshire and Goffstown reinvented themselves to take advantage of a new American trend: the rise of leisure time and the birth of the summer vacation.

Americans, particularly New Englanders, had always set aside Sunday as a day of rest, but until the middle of the nineteenth century, it was primarily intended as a day of religious observance and contemplation. People were expected to attend lengthy church services, read the Bible at home with their families and rest, just as the Bible claims God did on the seventh day of creation. As the nineteenth century progressed, though, Americans started to move away from this idea, mirroring a general movement toward a more secular society. Increasingly, then, Sunday became a day of true relaxation, when people wanted to forget about the duties and responsibilities that occupied them during the rest of the week and avoided lengthy contemplations on the state of their souls. Thus arose the idea of leisure time, a concept that did not really take off until industrialization and the rise of trade unions negotiated contracts for workers limiting the number of hours they could work in any one day or week. Factories were generally closed on Sundays, and by the end of the nineteenth century, some workers were even guaranteed Saturdays off, establishing the practice of the modern weekend.

Vacation time was another result of agreements between workers and bosses, although only the professional classes received it until well into the twentieth century. Nevertheless, more and more people began retreating from the cities in the summer months, be it for a day or for the whole summer, to enjoy the fresh air and scenic beauty of the countryside.

New Hampshire, and initially southern New Hampshire, quickly emerged as a prime vacation spot in New England. Far less developed than eastern Massachusetts, it was close enough to such big cities as Boston, Lowell and Lawrence to offer workers an opportunity to explore rural life without spending too long traveling to it. The expansion of rail lines and the introduction of electric trolleys, both of which occurred in the decades following the Civil War, made possible travel over long distances in a relatively short period of time.

At first, tourists stayed on people's farms, sometimes in their homes and sometimes in outbuildings that had been constructed or modified for their use. Gradually, the most successful of these farms (or the most enterprising of these farmers) built separate facilities for guests. In the northern part of the state, this was the era of the grand hotels, when promoters built massive resorts in the White Mountains that drew thousands of tourists every year. But the White Mountains were not the only region of New Hampshire to experience this tourism boom. Goffstown had its own grand hotels, beginning

A postcard of the Shirley Hill House. *Courtesy of the Goffstown Historical Society, Gerry Hart-Moss Collection.*

in 1870 with the construction of the Shirley Hill House on the south side of the Uncanoonucs.

Known for its panoramic views of the Merrimack Valley, the hotel was built by Shirley M. Johnson, a longtime Goffstown resident who was quick to recognize the potential of the state's tourism industry. With more than seventy rooms, his facility could house up to 250 people; it had a ballroom, restaurant, swimming pond and extensive grounds that spread over forty acres and included carriage trails. There was separate housing for the large staff that ran the hotel and catered to guests' every whim. It was considered a luxury hotel with such offerings as steam heating, electricity and artesian well water. The hotel organized day excursions to local spots of natural beauty like Pulpit Caverns in Bedford, Tipping Rock in Goffstown and even up to the top of the Uncanoonucs themselves, via a carriage road that had been built by the U.S. Coast Survey in 1850. The road had been taken over in 1877 by a group of local businessmen who formed the Uncanoonuc Road Company, which opened it for public use. A stagecoach, dubbed the "Tally-Ho," brought guests to the hotel from Shirley Station, where both the railroad and the electric trolley stopped. Only open between Memorial Day and Labor Day, the hotel housed some guests for the entire summer. Boston businessmen would set up their families there for the season and then travel up to be with them on the weekends. By the end of the nineteenth century, the Shirley Hill House was known as the largest and finest hotel in southern New Hampshire.

Goffstown had other offerings for tourists as well. In addition to the usual inns and taverns that grew up along well-traveled roads, there were numerous boardinghouses turned hotels. Mount Pleasant, on the north side of the Uncanoonucs, billed itself as a peaceful retreat with fresh mountain air, spectacular views, croquet and a swimming pond. Yacum Springs Hotel, on the south side of the Piscataquog River near Grasmere, had mineral springs and was run by two resident physicians, Drs. Charles and Albert George. The hotel offered clientele a treatment plan that would cure ills, promote good general health and lengthen life. Some claimed that an elixir developed by the George brothers could cure tuberculosis. Scribner's Mountain House, located in roughly the same area of Grasmere, was a massive six-story hotel with an observatory. Taggart's Hotel, a much older facility located within walking distance of Shirley Station, boasted a racetrack and stables that drew people from all over the region. The proprietor, David M. Taggart, also owned the nationally

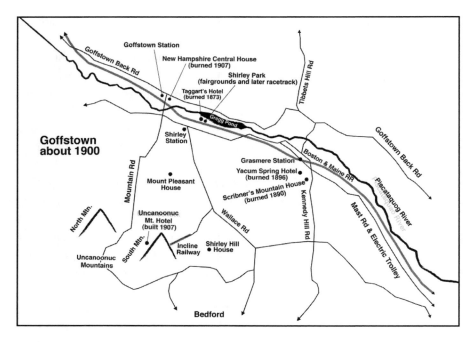

Goffstown about 1900 had a railroad, a trolley and an incline railroad, as well as several well-appointed hotels to accommodate out-of-town visitors. *Map created by Marshall Hudson.*

known racehorse Taggart's Abdallah, which was touted as the sire of the best family of trotting horses in New England.

Hotels and resorts proved to be just one component of Goffstown's tourism industry. With the lures of the Uncanoonucs and Gregg Pond (the forerunner of Glen Lake), Goffstown also became home to dozens of summer cottages. Many of these structures were built from scratch, but some were renovated farmhouses. The people who crowded into these usually small seasonal cabins produced a population explosion in town every summer, as hundreds of new residents spent their lazy summer days lounging around Goffstown. One large group of yearly visitors was of German origin. The group threw a grand picnic every year called the Glen Lake Festival, complete with food, music, singing, boat races, wrestling, games and, of course, beer. Having summer residents was typical of many New Hampshire towns, so much so that the state even began publishing and distributing an annual brochure, *New Hampshire Farms for Summer Homes*, listing abandoned farms for sale.

A postcard of Gregg Pond, the future Glen Lake, emphasizes its beauty and peacefulness. *Courtesy of the Goffstown Historical Society, Gerry Hart-Moss Collection.*

Given its proximity to Manchester, Goffstown also received visits from many day travelers. On their days off, workers from the Amoskeag Manufacturing Company would ride the trolley out to the rural countryside of nearby Goffstown to watch a horse race, hike a mountain or swim in the lake. Owned by the Manchester Street Railway, the trolley line reached Goffstown Village on July 24, 1900, running parallel with Mast Road and offering stops along the way. It was cheap and fast, thus providing an easy form of transportation and linking Manchester and Goffstown like never before.

Shortly after the turn of the twentieth century, Goffstown could boast another tourist attraction: an incline railroad that climbed to the top of South Uncanoonuc Mountain. The idea of building such a railroad originated in 1903 with a group of local businessmen. Before then, very little had been done with the South Mountain and nearly nothing at all with the North Mountain, which is actually sixteen feet higher. Farms ringed the base of each mountain, and the carriage road allowed access to the summit of the South Mountain. The U.S. Coast Survey had also built an observation tower at the summit in 1850 at the same time it had built the road, but that was all that had been established on the mountains

Sightseers arrive on the trolley at the base station for the incline railway. *Courtesy of the Goffstown Historical Society, Snay Collection.*

before the Uncanoonuc Incline Railway and Development Company was incorporated in 1903.

Over the next four years, the company constructed an electric railway that ran from the trolley stop at Shirley Station to a base station at the foot of the mountain; this portion was completed first and opened in 1905. It took two more years before passengers could transfer from the trolley to the incline railway, which took them to the top of the mountain. The incline railway covered a distance of 2,380 feet and ran at a 35 percent grade. Two rail cars ran on two separate tracks at a time, and they balanced each other, being linked by one cable measuring one and three-eighth inches that could support two hundred tons. When one car went up the mountain, the other one came down. The cars moved at a speed of twelve miles per hour. At 8 feet wide and 40 feet long, each car had a capacity of sixty people. Powered by two forty-horsepower motors, they were constructed with steel frames but wooden bodies. The whole system was designed and installed by the famed Otis Elevator Company.

Beginning on June 7, 1907, when the incline railway opened, passengers paid twenty-five cents for a round-trip ticket to the top of South

A postcard depicting the ride on the incline railway and the view of the valley below.
Courtesy of the Goffstown Historical Society, Snay Collection.

Uncanoonuc Mountain, which rose 1,348 feet above sea level. From there, visitors had an impressive view of four states (Mount Monadnock and Mount Washington in New Hampshire, the Bunker Hill Monument in Massachusetts, Mount Ascutney in Vermont and Mount Argamenticus in Maine). On a clear day, some people reported being able to see all the way to Boston Harbor.

The ascent also brought visitors to the new Uncanoonuc Mountain House, a grand hotel built at the summit of the mountain. Also owned by the Uncanoonuc Incline Railway and Development Company, the hotel was five stories high, with thirty-eight guest rooms, broad verandas on three sides so patrons could better enjoy the views, an observatory, a full offering of sporting activities (hiking, pool and billiards, picnic facilities, croquet, tennis and box bowling) and a lively dance pavilion that could hold eight hundred couples. In the pavilion, an orchestra played two nights per week and every Sunday afternoon through the summer months. The concerts were heavily promoted, particularly among the young crowd, under the slogan "Meet Me Under the Searchlight," which honored the twenty-thousand-kilowatt spotlight shining at night from the mountain's summit and into the surrounding countryside, sometimes even illuminating all the way to the Village. Each guest room contained

Sixty passengers could ride in each car of the incline railway. *Courtesy of the Goffstown Historical Society, Snay Collection.*

A postcard of the Uncanoonuc Mountain House. *Courtesy of the Goffstown Historical Society, Snay Collection.*

a private bathroom with hot and cold running water, a luxury indeed for this time period. The company also rented out forty-four summer cottages that dotted the mountain along either side of the incline railway. The railway, in fact, stopped at three platforms along its route to pick up and discharge passengers. In 1926, the company created a lake on the mountain, appropriately named Uncanoonuc Lake, covering twenty-four acres so that guests could boat, swim and fish. More than any other site, the facilities on the South Mountain made Goffstown a tourist attraction in the early part of the twentieth century, bringing thousands of people (both day-trippers and summer residents) to the town and establishing it as one of the best summer resorts in southern New Hampshire.

WINTER PEOPLE

G offstown's era of summer tourism came to an end in the 1920s, mainly because of the growing popularity of the automobile. As cars became cheaper and roads were paved, people began exploring farther on their own, no longer tied to railroad lines and timetables. Summer tourists still came to Goffstown, especially to the cabins around the lake (which had been renamed Glen Lake in 1917 after a new dam had been constructed enlarging Gregg Pond), but they no longer came in the overwhelming numbers they had before World War I.

In place of summer tourism, though, a new industry arose: winter tourism. Beginning in the early 1930s, New Englanders developed a fascination with downhill skiing, and many of the features that had made the South Mountain an attractive summer retreat now made it an equally attractive winter one. For example, although automobiles had become popular for summer travel, people were still hesitant to travel long distances by car in winter weather, concerned about the safety and maneuverability of cars on snow and ice. Traditional sleighs remained so popular that until 1927 the town only plowed one side of the main streets after a snow storm for use by cars. The other side was packed down by an enormous roller pulled by horses to allow sleighs to travel through town.

Until well into the 1920s, many people continued to store their cars during the winter months and travel exclusively by sleigh. Therefore, trains and trolleys still provided an important source of transportation for people looking to take a vacation in the winter months, one that didn't require them to shovel

This giant roller packed the snow on the roads so that sleighs could travel more easily in the winter. After 1927, the roads were plowed for automobiles rather than rolled for sleighs. *Courtesy of the Goffstown Historical Society, Gerry Hart-Moss Collection.*

snow or drive in icy conditions. Once again, the Uncanoonucs' proximity to major urban areas made it a convenient spot for weekend getaways, complete with high-quality accommodations found at the Shirley Hill House or the Uncanoonuc Mountain House. And the incline railway, which had begun to fall out of use for sightseers, was an outstanding method of getting skiers to the top of the mountain, particularly as ski lifts were in their infancy at this point. Other mountainous locations around New Hampshire also began to cultivate reputations for skiing, and many of them offered more glamorous locations and more challenging slopes in the White Mountains, but for convenience, Goffstown could not be beat. It became the largest ski resort in southern New Hampshire.

People had been skiing in New England since the 1870s. The sport had been brought over to the United States by Scandinavian immigrants hired to build a railroad in northern New England in the 1850s. Thirty families settled outside of Berlin, New Hampshire, in an area that came to be known as Norway Village. In 1872, they began a ski club, but it mostly focused on cross-country skiing and jumping, which had been popular in their native land. Other New Englanders eventually embraced these sports, particularly at Dartmouth College, where students initiated their own ski club in 1909.

In the early part of the 1920s, downhill skiing became popular in Europe and soon made its way to America. New Englanders took to it instantly and in far greater numbers than had ever embraced cross-country skiing or jumping. By 1925, the Dartmouth Outing Club had built its first slalom course. The following year, the first competitive downhill race in the United States was held at Mount Moosilauke in the White Mountains of New Hampshire. In the early 1930s, the Civilian Conservation Corps and the Works Project Administration, organizations established during the Great Depression to provide work for unemployed laborers, began to cut or widen trails on New Hampshire mountainsides, opening up more areas for skiing. Summer resorts around the state began to stay open year-round to accommodate New Englanders' newest passion.

Goffstown was part of this boom. In 1931, the newly formed Uncanoonuc Ski Club began cutting its own trails on the mountains, the first one being the Dorsey Trail on the North Mountain. The trail was named in honor of Herbert G. Dorsey, an arctic geologist from Washington, D.C., who introduced the idea of downhill skiing to Goffstown. In 1935, a few years after the trail opened, Dorsey went with Admiral Richard E. Byrd on an expedition to the South Pole. By then, Goffstown had eight trails open for skiing, and the Boston & Maine Railroad had begun running special excursions called snow trains to Goffstown, bringing in about 1,000 people per day on two trains for just $1.75 per round-trip ticket. The incline railway flourished. For $0.50 a ride, skiers could reach the top of the South Mountain in a matter of minutes, saving themselves a two-hour hike by foot up the old carriage road. At the height of Goffstown's skiing craze in 1936 and 1937, roughly 1,200 people a day were riding the incline railway to the slopes. All of these efforts received a tremendous amount of promotion from various organizations in town, including such newly formed groups as the Goffstown Outing Club and the Goffstown Chamber of Commerce. Those backing the ski industry in Goffstown had high hopes and billed the area as the "St. Moritz of America."

Sadly, the town's new tourist industry collapsed almost as quickly as it had begun, felled by a series of natural disasters. The massive hurricane of 1938, which wreaked such havoc throughout New England, destroyed both the Uncanoonuc Mountain House and the Shirley Hill House. Neither facility was rebuilt. The Boston & Maine halted passenger service on the line that same year. Even the popularity of the snow trains could not offset the declining ridership that had plagued the railroad since World War I. Three years later, in 1941, a fire consumed a large stretch of the incline railway. Although it was repaired, another fire damaged it badly shortly thereafter. The railway was sold for scrap and dismantled in 1949.

The Goffstown Chamber of Commerce distributed brochures highlighting Goffstown's year-round attractions. *Courtesy of the Goffstown Historical Society.*

Some Goffstown entrepreneurs tried to keep the skiing industry alive, albeit on a much smaller scale. They built tow ropes and T-bars on the mountains and opened their own small ski slopes, but none of these efforts came even close to producing the volume of tourists that had come to town in the mid-1930s. By the time World War II ended, New Englanders had begun to travel to the White Mountains for their winter recreation, and only locals used the ski trails in town. By the 1960s, even those had fallen into disuse, and skiing in Goffstown came to an end.

GOFFSTOWN BECOMES A SUBURB

The end of World War II ushered in a period of great change in Goffstown and the nation, just as the end of the Revolutionary War and the Civil War had done. Many people are familiar with most of those changes: the baby boom, the prevalence of automobiles and electric appliances and the triumph of middle-class prosperity. All of these changes were reflected in the life of Goffstown. Added to them was Goffstown's greatest challenge yet—its relegation to being a suburb of Manchester and the resulting vulnerability of its own sense of community.

Although Manchester's predecessor, Derryfield, had been founded before Goffstown, Goffstown quickly surpassed it in population and influence. Within a few short years after its incorporation, Goffstown had become one of the principal towns in Hillsborough County. Even when Manchester began experiencing population booms due to the influx of workers to the Amoskeag Mills, Goffstown retained a position of importance within the county, containing such essential county facilities as the poorhouse, hospital and jail. It was also the primary commercial center on the west bank of the Merrimack River and served as a business focal point and gateway for all the people living farther west in the county. Yet as Manchester grew exponentially in size in the nineteenth century, it also grew in influence until it eventually overshadowed all the towns in New Hampshire's Merrimack Valley.

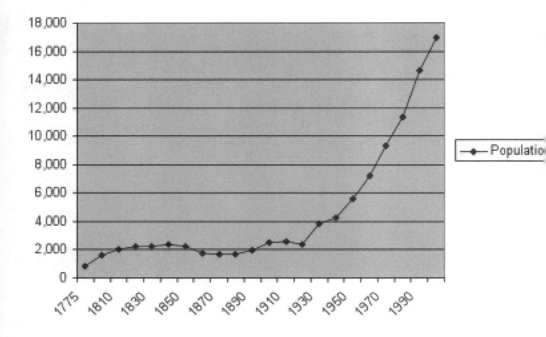

Table 1. Goffstown Population by Year

1775	1800	1810	1820	1830	1840	1850	1860	1870	1880	1890
831	1,612	2,000	2,230	2,213	2,376	2,270	1,740	1,656	1,699	1,981
1900	1910	1920	1930	1940	1950	1960	1970	1980	1990	2000
2,528	2,579	2,381	3,839	4,247	5,638	7,230	9,284	11,315	14,621	16,929

By the early part of the twentieth century, Goffstown had lost much
of its importance in county affairs, but it still retained a strong sense
of community—a palpable feeling that the town was a unique place,
despite the arrival of large groups of immigrants in town. Neither the
advent of the railroad and the trolley nor the bridge between Pinardville
and Manchester's West Side, all of which linked the two towns so firmly,

could shake Goffstown's view of itself. This idea that everyone in town was somehow connected to everyone else was reinforced by the town's size. With a population of fewer than four thousand in 1930, people in town knew just about everyone else, and residents at the time claimed that all families were linked in some manner or another. The police force consisted of just one officer, and the fire department in the Village was manned by workers from the nearby Kendall-Hadley factory, whose whistle served as the town's fire alarm. The switchboard operator, who was responsible for manually placing all telephone calls in the days of crank phones, was a woman named Edith Hart, and everyone in town knew her voice well. The town's newest park, Barnard Park (built in the 1920s), had a grand bandstand to hold the people who turned out en masse to watch the town's much-hailed baseball team, the Goffstown Ghosts, and their star player, Bill Whipple. In short, Goffstown still had a small-town feel to it.

Between 1940 and 1950, though, the population began to shoot upward at a much faster pace, and Goffstown began to feel less like a small integrated community and more like a suburb of Manchester. Many of the old farmsteads were sold to developers, who built single-family homes by the dozens in a trend that would continue right into the twenty-first century. More homes were created when people began buying up the old summer cottages and winterizing them for year-round use. Mast Road in Pinardville emerged as a new commercial center in town, one that was lined with strip malls, gas stations and fast-food restaurants.

So what fueled this demographic shift in the middle of the twentieth century, especially as the Manchester mills had closed their doors in 1935? Why did Goffstown become a suburb just when Manchester was at its most vulnerable? The answer is in part because of Manchester's vulnerability. With factory jobs disappearing, people were no longer tied to Manchester and began seeking opportunities in the surrounding communities. Conversely, after several years of economic struggle, Manchester itself began to offer new opportunities for people in light industries as companies like Raytheon moved into the area. Manchester's importance as the largest city in northern New England also kept people in the area. In the latter decades of the twentieth century, Manchester also enjoyed some residual benefit from the technological revolution that occurred farther south, along Route 128 in Massachusetts.

Many of the people lured to the Merrimack Valley by Manchester's economic possibilities, though, did not want to live in an urban setting. In fact, perhaps the most significant factor leading to the suburbanization of Goffstown was cultural. Beginning in World War II, Americans began to

A postcard showing an idyllic vision of Goffstown Village. *Courtesy of the Goffstown Historical Society, Gerry Hart-Moss Collection.*

romanticize New England village life like never before. Fueled by numerous articles in the national press, the depiction in film and books of the "typical" American town that could only have been modeled after towns in New England and the popularity of the artist Norman Rockwell with his charming idealizations of New England town life, New England villages came forcefully back into vogue. They became, in effect, the American ideal, and suddenly everyone wanted to live in a small rural community with a village green and a white-steepled church.

Southern New Hampshire became a particularly popular destination once again, in part because of its proximity to Boston but also because it was relatively undeveloped (when compared to southern New England) and because the state had such low taxes. The result was a full-scale population shift, led by people from Massachusetts who sought a simpler, more affordable lifestyle in New Hampshire. The region's promise brought people from the rest of the country, too. Between 1960 and 1970, New Hampshire experienced a population gain of more than 20 percent, which was nearly twice the national average.

To towns all over southern New Hampshire, the new arrivals brought money, youth and energy. With an influx of young families, the demographic shift reversed the state's trend toward an aging population against which it had been struggling since the late nineteenth century. Tax revenues went up, but so did the need for additional town services, from new roads and sewers to expanded schools to increased emergency personnel. Town governments struggled to keep up, as the real estate market boomed and new construction arose at an incredible speed.

The new arrivals also presented a quandary for the towns. With so many people coming in from so many different places at such incredible speed, how did the towns avoid being lumped together as one giant suburb of Manchester—or worse, a somewhat distant suburb of Boston? With so many older structures being torn down to make way for new ones, how did any town have a chance of preserving its heritage? Each town responded in its own way, but many embraced their local history as the surest means of protecting those features that originally made them unique. Local efforts corresponded to state and national efforts to celebrate all aspects of history, from the deeds of the famous to the everyday lifestyles of average Americans.

In mid-century, Goffstown seized the chance to promote its own history through a series of events. First, the town commemorated the bicentennial of its incorporation in 1961 with a grand weeklong celebration that followed a pattern similar to the original Old Home Week celebrations. Dinners, speeches, a historical pageant, a baseball game, concerts, a parade, church services and a firemen's muster were all scheduled for the week, as well as new events like special train rides to Manchester, open houses at various buildings, fireworks, a carnival, a ball and an arts and crafts festival.

The celebration sparked a new interest in the town's history that culminated in the founding of the Goffstown Historical Society in 1969 and its acquisition of the old Parker Store in 1972. With a museum open to the public several times throughout the year and a collection of town documents and artifacts, the historical society became the keeper of the town's heritage, not least because so many of its members have a lifetime of experience with Goffstown.

Just a few years later, the town celebrated the national bicentennial with another round of festivities similar to those held in 1961. The town's Heritage Quilt was created in that same year of 1976. The quilt is a hand-stitched representation of the town's history through forty sixteen-inch squares with one large center square portraying the Village. The project was a massive effort by more than fifty volunteers, many of whom worked in family groups to create their squares, sometimes with the participation of several generations. The finished quilt won many awards and was featured

The center panel of the Heritage Quilt.

in the March 1978 issue of *Good Housekeeping* magazine after being named one of ten finalists in a nationwide contest. Today, it hangs in the Goffstown Historical Society.

Goffstown also embraced the relatively new idea of establishing local historic districts in the 1980s, when town voters approved new zoning ordinances to grant special protection to properties in three newly proclaimed historic districts: the Parker Station area, two homes on Carr Court off the south common of the Village and the central portion of Grasmere around the Grasmere Town Hall. Zoned specifically for historic preservation and with the help of property owners in each district, these areas are intended to capture an image of the town's heritage for future generations.

Transformations of a New England Town

Except for the creation of the Heritage Quilt, which was a completely unique event, all the efforts to protect local history were also happening in other towns in southern New Hampshire, as nearly everyone wrestled with the same problem—assimilating the new arrivals to the region and helping them feel invested in the communities to which they had moved. But another factor encouraging historic preservation and the protection of New England's towns and villages was the resurgence of the state's tourism industry. Not everyone could pick up and move to rural New Hampshire, no matter how badly they yearned for New England village life and the American ideal. For most people, a visit to those villages, particularly when the autumn colors of a New Hampshire fall painted the landscape, would have to suffice. Although tourists had always come to New Hampshire for the stunning scenery, the second half of the twentieth century saw the arrival of more weekend leaf-peepers than ever, a trend once again fueled by an improved transportation system, this time in the form of a good highway system. By 1970, tourism had become the second largest industry in the state, generating millions of dollars of revenue every year. The arrival of this wave of tourism emphasized the importance of maintaining each town's heritage. The leaf-peepers came not only to see the array of colors on the trees but also to see the charming New England villages they had seen depicted in magazines, television shows and movies. This trend continues unabated today.

THE GIANT PUMPKINS
ARE COMING!

Much of the effort to preserve New England villages centered on their downtown areas. After all, this is where the town commons and the white-steepled churches were located. If residents were to have a central meeting place to reinforce their sense of community, and if tourists were to have some place to get meals and buy souvenirs, the commercial districts had to be charming, picturesque and vibrant business areas.

In Goffstown in the late twentieth century, that effort focused on the Village, which had been the town's economic and social center for well over one hundred years. Main Street had once been touted as a beautiful, wide street, lined with grand elm trees and home to a lively business community. The Opera House served as an important meeting place for the townspeople, hosting countless programs that brought folks into town on a regular basis. With the town's main factories grouped in or near the Village, and the vast majority of its businesses located there, it was truly the heart and soul of the community.

By the middle of the twentieth century, though, much of that had changed. The Opera House's destruction by fire in March 1937 left the town without a town hall in the Village for nearly ten years. Although a new town hall was built in 1947, it did not have the large meeting spaces that the Opera House had offered, thus depriving the town of a place to host community events. The trolleys that once ran down Mast Road

The Gove House of 1805. *Courtesy of the Goffstown Historical Society, Gerry Hart-Moss Collection.*

had been replaced by busses in 1938, but even these stopped running in Goffstown in 1971. And perhaps most damaging to the Village district was people's increasing tendency to drive to Manchester to run their errands and do their shopping.

Inevitably, Main Street itself fell into a decline. With no oversight or central planning, the area had become a jumble of buildings, spanning a broad range of architectural styles from colonial to modern. In the early 1990s, there was very little that was picturesque about it. Some important landmarks had been lost, too. The stately Gove House, which dated back to 1805, was replaced by the more modern St. Lawrence Church in 1965. Also, Goffstown's famous covered railroad bridge had burned down in August 1976. Both of the parks in the Village area—the town common that had been built in 1907 and a small area that had been filled in and constructed in the space between the old train bridge and the car bridge in 1968—were also in need of expansion and repair.

Nevertheless, there were some impressive buildings along Main Street. The homes around the south common in particular were some of the most beautiful houses in town, despite the fact that most of them had been converted to apartments. The town hall, which had been remodeled in 1970 to both look more attractive and be more functional, looked just as a New England building should, as did the Congregational church and Memorial Library, which anchored the north end of the district. Some individual

The covered railroad bridge in the Village burned down on August 16, 1976. *Courtesy of the Goffstown Historical Society, Grant Collection.*

Some residents referred to the new town hall (built in 1947) as "the aircraft carrier" because of its flat roof. *Courtesy of the Goffstown Historical Society, Gerry Hart-Moss Collection.*

property owners had worked hard to keep their buildings attractive, but others lacked the funds or the drive to do so. Altogether, the downtown district was limping along by the late 1990s, with a few thriving businesses and many more barely surviving.

But that was all about to change. In 1998, a group of business owners formed a steering committee to investigate ways to revitalize the downtown area. A new effort was about to get underway, and they were determined to assist with it. A group of citizens had decided to enlarge and re-landscape the town common, turning it into a more useful and appealing outdoor meeting space for the community.

Another effort the committee decided to pursue was membership in the New Hampshire Main Street Program. Supported at the state level, the Main Street Program focuses on revitalization of downtown communities for its members. It has a trademarked four-point approach that each designated Main Street community must follow. The approach involves organizing property and business owners, government officials and civic leaders to work together to keep the downtown vibrant; promoting community events to draw people to the downtown district; improving the visual attractiveness of the downtown through a design structure compatible with the historic character of the area; and helping district businesspeople find an economic mix that works for the community. The steering committee's application to be designated a Main Street community was accepted in the spring of 1999, and the group quickly appointed its first director, Robbie Grady.

In a matter of months, Grady and the board of directors for the new organization opened an office, joined in the effort to renovate the town common and had begun planning their first significant event, a fall festival held in October that would coincide with the rededication of the common. The festival was a success, and a resource team from the statewide Main Street organization suggested that the Goffstown group make the fall festival its signature event.

A member of the Main Street board, Jim Beauchemin suggested tying the fall festival to a pumpkin regatta. Other communities, including one in Massachusetts, had held such events with success. Also, several giant pumpkin growers were from Goffstown and the surrounding communities. Beauchemin was a giant pumpkin grower himself. The idea was that four giant pumpkins (generously donated by their growers) would be hollowed out and small outboard motors attached to their backs. The "boats" would be piloted by well-known figures from the town who would race their pumpkins down the river. Beauchemin then suggested the board add an additional element by inviting the New Hampshire Giant Pumpkin Growers Association to make the festival its official weigh-in.

The first year of the newly named Pumpkin Regatta and Weigh-In was held over two weekends in October 2000. During the first weekend, twenty-one pumpkins were weighed in by the New Hampshire Growers on a crisp,

From left to right is Fire Chief Ed Hunter, Police Chief Mike French and Main Street's Jim Beauchemin in the first Pumpkin Regatta. *Courtesy of the Goffstown Main Street Program.*

clear, perfect New England fall day. There were a number of other activities organized for the day as well, with various clubs selling food, a variety of games and activities for kids and a parade with a pumpkin prince and princess. Close to 1,500 people turned out for the festivities in the first true community celebration Goffstown had seen in years.

By the following weekend, though, the weather had turned. The day of the regatta dawned cold and stormy, with snow flurries falling intermittently. The honor of driving the boats had already been awarded to four groups: the board of selectmen (represented by Chairwoman Barbara Griffin), the police department (Chief Mike French), the fire department (Chief Ed Hunter) and the Main Street Program (Jim Beauchemin). If any of the participants had been reluctant to take part in the race, they did a good job of hiding it. All four showed up in costume for the event, with some decorations for their pumpkins as well. The selectmen's pumpkin had even been painted bright pink. All four participants also came armed with Super Soaker water guns. With snow flakes falling, the race commenced but turned into something of a mêlée when a surprise contestant entered at the end. Another Main Street member, Bob McKinnon, had constructed a pirate ship out of a barge that motored in toward the end of the race and began chasing down the other boats. Despite the damp and cold, the regatta

Barbara Griffin represented the board of selectmen dressed as a princess in a pumpkin painted bright pink in the first Pumpkin Regatta. *Courtesy of the Goffstown Main Street Program.*

Bob McKinnon's pirate boat. *Courtesy of the Goffstown Main Street Program.*

was declared a success, with five to six hundred people turning out to watch the event, even in the snow. In future years, the activities would be compressed into a single weekend, but many of the traditions established during this first festival would remain.

The Pumpkin Regatta and Weigh-In has since become a much-beloved feature of Goffstown life. By the end of the decade, nearly three thousand people were turning out for the festival, many of them traveling from some distance for it, their interest piqued by reports from Goffstown family or friends. Despite the festival's success, it has remained very much a local event, just as the organizers from Main Street intended. All the vendors and merchants operating at the festival are local, and many local groups take advantage of the opportunity offered by the community celebration to showcase their accomplishments.

The Main Street Program can boast of other contributions to the community as well. It has either reintroduced or established a whole program of events in the Village, including Old Home Day, a summer concert series, Halloween and Christmas festivities and an art show. It has also established a grant program to help beautify the district and make it more accessible to residents, all of which serve to help distinguish Goffstown from other towns and to reinforce residents' sense of community. Other changes to Main Street have come in these years as well. The little park near the old train bridge was adopted by the Rotary Club, which re-landscaped it and added a fountain. Several storefronts have been remodeled, and the hardware store, the largest commercial business in town, built a large new facility just off Main Street, allowing it to expand its operations significantly. The Main Street Program has been a part of many of these changes.

Among the program's most recent accomplishments was its cooperation with the Goffstown Historic District Commission to list the Village on the National Register of Historic Places as a national historic district. The Village reflects nearly two hundred years in the history of a New England town and is still the center of the town's vibrant community life.

THE NEW VILLA AUGUSTINA

O ther groups in town were also facing challenges in the first years of the twenty-first century. Many of the service organizations and civic groups confronted aging memberships, underscored by the lack of new recruits. This problem was felt most keenly in the town government, where committee appointments routinely went unfilled and various boards operated with only the bare minimum of members, hampered by a lack of volunteers willing to donate their time and expertise to the community. With the hectic pace of the late twentieth and early twenty-first centuries, most townspeople had other things to do with their time than serve in town government or join a service organization.

In 2007, it looked as if a Goffstown institution would close for just this reason. The sisters of the Religious of Jesus and Mary (RJMs), who ran the Villa Augustina school on Mast Road, had begun closing schools across the country, citing a lack of members to keep these facilities operating. The RJMs had faced a dramatic loss of numbers in the second half of the twentieth century, with only one-third of the number of sisters in 2004 that it had had in 1955. The average age of the RJMs was rising, too, prompting concerns about caring for the increasingly elderly population of sisters. With more missions and schools operating in very poor countries like Haiti, India and Pakistan, the loss of numbers forced the provincial office to reevaluate its efforts. The result was a shift of focus for the order: the RJMs would scale back their educational pursuits in the United States in an effort to preserve their missions abroad. Many Catholic schools run by religious orders not

A postcard of the Villa viewed from across Glen Lake. *Courtesy of the Goffstown Historical Society, Grant Collection.*

officially designated diocesan schools (and thereby not financially supported by the diocese) were in similar circumstances. There were simply too many people in the world who needed their services and not enough priests and nuns to help. Thus throughout the last decades of the twentieth century, American Catholic schools had been closing at an alarming rate. A great number of those schools, some sources say as many as three hundred, had been operated by the RJMs.

In most cases, the schools simply closed. But in a few cases, parents attempted to save the schools, something that happened at the Villa. When the sisters announced the impending closing of the school at a meeting in December 2007, parents responded with an overwhelming show of support. They offered both their time and money to keep the school open, even if it meant the parents had to run it themselves. The event was well covered in the local media, but few people seemed to realize just how remarkable the school's transition was. Of all the Catholic schools facing closure in the United States in recent years, only Villa Augustina successfully made the jump to a parent-run organization, independent of the religious order that had founded the school.

Villa Augustina had long been a feature of the Goffstown landscape. The large, brick building occupied a prominent location on Mast Road, and over the years, the school had educated thousands of students, including many

An early twentieth-century postcard depicting perhaps the Villa of the future. *Courtesy of the Goffstown Historical Society, Grant Collection.*

from Goffstown. It was founded during the very years that Edmond Pinard launched his development effort in Pinardville to bring French-Canadians to the town. Anxious to preserve their own culture and concerned that their children's education in public schools would be hampered by their unfamiliarity with English, many French-Canadians were enthusiastic about a school that would embrace their heritage. Manchester already had two such schools: the Académie Saint-Augustin, which was a boys' school founded in 1889, and the Académie Notre-Dame, which was a girls' school founded in 1903 but based on a much older French-Canadian establishment.

Between 1903 and 1905, several Catholic figures associated with the RJMs or working with them suggested that they establish a new facility, this one outside of Manchester. Its purpose would be twofold: to educate French-Canadian girls who lived in the surrounding countryside and to establish a recreational retreat for the RJMs. In 1907, led by the superior at the Académie Notre-Dame, Mère St. Honoré, the sisters bought the Daniel Little farm in Goffstown, a 125-acre spread nestled at the base of the Uncanoonucs. The old farmhouse was renovated and opened as a convent the following year.

With the retreat established, the sisters next turned their attention to raising funds for the new school. Finally, in 1916, construction crews broke ground, and two years later, on September 5, 1918, the new school opened its doors for students. The Villa was a girls' boarding school and offered instruction for grades one through twelve. Half of the subjects were taught in French (with courses in religion, the history of France and Canada, art, gym and a series of home arts) and half in English (with courses in literature, Latin, history, mathematics and the sciences). Over the years, the school enjoyed steady growth, gaining a reputation for academic rigorousness and small class sizes. In 1968, it underwent two major changes. First, it stopped giving instruction in grades nine through twelve, maintaining that the other high schools in the area, including the three Catholic high schools, were adequate for the community's needs. Second, it went co-ed. Most of the students were day students by that time anyway, and the school converted to all day students a few years later. In 1989, the school created a school board to assist the sisters in its operation. By 2002, the school was operating at capacity, with well over three hundred students and a waiting list. It maintained its reputation for high academic standards and was one of the few private elementary schools in New Hampshire to be accredited by the New England Association of Schools and Colleges, a much coveted honor.

At roughly the same time, though, the physical condition of the school's primary building became a source of concern. Given its age, it was in need of significant renovation, and by 2005, some parents had begun to speculate that the RJMs might opt to close the school rather than invest substantial sums of money in it. With the national organization struggling and rumors of the Villa's possible closing, parents began to pull their children and enroll them in other Catholic schools in the Manchester area, causing enrollment to decline.

A handful of parents, mostly those who were already volunteering substantial amounts of time at the school, suspected by late 2006 that the school's impending closure was more than a rumor. The school board paid little heed, not believing the school was in any real danger of closing. Quietly, some parents, working independently and in small groups, began gathering information about just what it would take to keep the school open if the RJMs no longer ran it.

Suddenly, at a hastily called parents meeting on December 12, 2007, Sister Janet Stolba, the provincial superior of the RJMs, announced that the school would close in June, in part because a recently commissioned feasibility study had shown the enormous amount of money required for necessary repairs to the building. Most parents were stunned by the news. Even the sisters who worked at the school had not known in advance. Rather than reacting with anger about the school's closing, though, a remarkable number of parents rallied and vowed to save it. It helped that the parents who had suspected the closing was coming had already begun investigating what was involved in keeping the school open. Also, the consultant who had prepared the feasibility study announced that from what he had seen of the Villa community while working on the study, he believed it was capable of raising the funds for the repairs, even though the task would be enormous. By the end of the night, the parents had convinced Sister Janet to give them time to organize and put together a plan for the transfer of the school. She gave them one week.

Within a matter of days, the parents had elected a five-person interim board to orchestrate the transition. Parents with a variety of skills stepped forward to offer their services in saving the school, from accountants and lawyers to engineers and teachers. Nearly all the parents who had been investigating options to save the school came together and agreed to work with the transition board in one collective effort. Members of the board began to hold informal discussions with Sister Janet about the possibility of selling the school to them.

As a result, on December 21, the RJMs outlined their proposal for the transfer of the school in a ten-point document that laid out a series of mandates. Many of the mandates had to do with the necessary repairs to the building and the creation of a governance structure for the new school, but chief among the directives was a selling price of $400,000 for the school and thirty-three surrounding acres. In addition, the document stipulated that by the end of June 2008 the connection between the RJMs and the school would be severed.

The transition board more or less agreed to the terms and began the daunting assignment of implementing each mandate. It was no small task these parents had set for themselves. They had to create from scratch an entirely new organization to take over the running of the school, and then they had to run it. They also had to raise enormous sums of money in a very brief period of time to buy the school from the RJMs while conducting a number of vital repairs that the sisters had not been able to do in past years. The job also involved a dramatic change in the role that parents played in school affairs. Under the RJMs, parental involvement had been fairly limited in the school's administration. Although parents were encouraged to volunteer in the classroom or the front office while helping to raise auxiliary funds through the parent-teacher association (called Home and School), the sisters had maintained a firm grip over the actual running of the school; parents were generally not consulted in administrative matters. All that changed when parents decided to take over the school for themselves. Keeping it open would require parents to become involved in school affairs as they never had been before. And all this had to be accomplished in just a little over six months.

The most pressing matter was raising the necessary funds, both for the repairs and the purchase price. To administer the fundraising effort, the transition board formed a new nonprofit corporation called Villa Future, adopting the slogan "Believe!" The entire capital campaign received a boost when just days after the sisters had sent their proposal, an anonymous donor contributed $100,000 to the effort, promising another $200,000 if the parents could match it. With this show of encouragement, more donations began coming in, even from people with no connection to the Villa other than a desire to see it succeed. A few weeks later, another anonymous donor gave an additional $100,000, and the monks at Saint Anselm College contributed a further $100,000. Other fundraising efforts were smaller but contributed to the energy of the campaign, with one high schooler and Villa alumna donating her savings account. The school also received numerous small donations of just a few dollars from people with no connection to the school but who had read about its predicament in the newspaper. Bishop Brady High School in Concord, where many Villa graduates attended grades nine through twelve, began a button-selling campaign, with buttons bearing "Believe!" going for $2. The transition board also negotiated a loan from St. Mary's Bank on very favorable terms to secure sufficient funds.

Money was not the only issue, though. The transition board had to contend with a host of legal issues, including the establishment of a new organization to actually administer the school. Of great emotional impact was the school's new name, which had to change with the new organization. The board selected St. Claudine Villa Academy, after the RJMs' founder, a nineteenth-century French nun named Claudine Thévenet. As a final gift to the school, though, the sisters granted their permission for the school to continue operating under the name by which it was commonly known, Villa Augustina.

Of nearly as much concern as the fundraising effort was the problem of enrollment. Although the level of support among most of the parents was phenomenal, some parents panicked and either pulled their children from the school shortly after the December meeting or made other arrangements for the following school year. The school had begun the 2007–08 school year with more than 250 students, but by the end of that same year, it had just under 200 pupils still attending. In an effort to stem the tide and show its support for the Villa, the Manchester diocese ordered a moratorium on enrolling former Villa students at its schools, a directive that not all of the schools honored. In response to the falling enrollment, the transition board implemented a new financial aid policy, which allowed more families to afford a Villa education than ever before.

The smaller enrollment, though, meant less operating funds for the school just at the very time it needed such funds the most. Although an effort was made to retain a great number of the faculty, many of whom had become beloved institutions at the school in their own right, some members of the staff had to be let go. The school's leadership also underwent a complete change, not only because of the creation of the new governance structure but also because of the arrival of a new principal, Charles Lawrence.

By the end of June 2008, the transition board oversaw the purchase of the school and the transfer of governance to the newly created school board. Remarkably, the parents had met all the requirements laid out by the sisters just six months before, and the Villa had become an independent Catholic school run by a lay organization. It had been, as supporters were fond of saying, a "year of miracles" for the Villa community. But despite the phenomenal accomplishment of saving the school, its future is by no means secure, as the school strives to recover from its tumultuous transition.

EPILOGUE

If this story seems to end abruptly, it's because the story isn't really over. The saga of Villa Augustina is simply the most recent example of a Goffstown community reinventing itself. Now, as Goffstown prepares to celebrate the 250th anniversary of the adoption of its charter in 2011, it appears to be on the verge of reinventing itself yet again. In recent years, several organizations have promoted projects that promise to bring business to the community and reinforce the townspeople's bonds with one another.

Collectively the effort is beginning to take shape under the title "Destination Goffstown." Initiated by the town's Economic Development Council in 2008, the group seeks to develop and promote a wide range of resources that will make Goffstown an entertaining destination, both for those of us who live here and for visitors from other communities. Some of the projects currently underway include:

- the completion of the Rail Trail (a 5.5-mile biking and walking path in the rail bed of the old B&M Railroad)
- the promotion of the river as a source of recreation with water activities like boating, canoeing, kayaking, swimming and fishing, along with the boat launches, rental facilities and beaches to support them
- a renewed interest in the mountains, both because of the trails that crisscross them and the idea that they could again be used for winter recreational sports like tubing

- the development of the John Stark Scenic Byway, which runs through New Boston, Weare and Dunbarton but begins and ends in Goffstown Village and includes several scenic locations, gift shops, antique stores and a few restaurants
- the establishment of a major town park, complete with ball fields, a gazebo for community events, picnic areas and a playground
- the renovation of Grasmere Town Hall, with its 225-person theatre on the second floor, promising indoor entertainment such as classes, recitals, plays, concerts, movies, lectures or anything else the townspeople want to organize, as well as serving as a community meeting place

All of these features are supported by local groups composed of volunteers who donate their time to enrich the social life of the community and strengthen the bonds that tie people together. Destination Goffstown is the way the town is reinventing itself at this moment, and it is a way that should be more or less familiar to those who know something of Goffstown's history. Remarkably, many people are unaware that Goffstown was one of the premier recreational destinations in New Hampshire not so many decades ago. Will this be the last time the town reinvents itself? Most definitely not, if history is any guide to the future. The only thing that is assured is that in some form or another Goffstown will certainly be reborn.

SOURCES

I have listed below some of the most helpful and noted resources for both Goffstown and New Hampshire history. By no means does this list represent the extent of my sources. The "Goffstown" portion of this list includes all the major treatments of the town's history, although some of them are quite dated.

GOFFSTOWN

Bacon, George F. *Manchester and Its Leading Businessmen Embracing Also Those of Goffstown*. Boston: Mercantile Publishing Co., 1891.

Batchellor, Albert Stillman, ed. *New Hampshire State Papers*. Vol. 24, *Town Charters*. Concord, NH: Edward N. Pearson, 1894.

———. *New Hampshire State Papers*. Vol. 25, *Town Charters*. Concord, NH: Edward N. Pearson, 1895.

Blood, Grace Holbrook. *Manchester on the Merrimack: The Story of a City*. Manchester, NH: Manchester Historical Association, 1975.

Bouton, Nathaniel, ed. *Documents and Records Relating to Towns in New Hampshire*. Vol. 9. Concord, NH: Charles C. Pearson, 1875.

SOURCES

Brown, William Howard. *Colonel John Goffe: Eighteenth Century New Hampshire.* Manchester, NH: Lew A. Cummings Co., 1950.

Carr, Alonzo. "History of Goffstown." In *History of Hillsborough County*, compiled by D. Hamilton Hurd. Philadelphia: J.W. Lewis, 1885.

Daniell, Jere R. "The New England Town and Goffstown," a lecture in honor of Old Home Day, 2008.

Goffstown New Hampshire Bi-Centennial, 1761–1961. Goffstown, NH, 1961.

Gove, Douglas Earle. *Memory Bank: Recollections of Goffstown, New Hampshire.* N.p.: self-published, 1998.

———. *Memory Bank II: Recollections of New Hampshire People.* N.p.: self-published, 2000.

———. *Memory Bank III: Recollections of Goffstown People.* N.p.: self-published, 2004.

Hadley, George Plummer. *History of the Town of Goffstown, 1733–1920.* 2 vols. Concord, NH: Rumford Press, 1922.

Hammond, Isaac. *Documents Relating to Towns in New Hampshire.* Vol. 12. Concord, NH: Parsons B. Cogswell, 1883.

Heritage Quilt: Goffstown Bicentennial, 1776–1976. Concord, NH: Bridge & Byron, 1976.

McKeon, Valerie. "The Founding of Saint Anselm College: New Hampshire's First Catholic College." *Historical New Hampshire* 41 (Spring/Summer 1986): 21–44.

"Old Home Day Exercises." Goffstown, NH, September 1904.

Perreault, Robert. "Keeping Alive the Dream: A History of Villa Augustina School." Unpublished work, 1993.

Pierce, Richard D. "Historical Address delivered October 26th, 1941 in the Congregational Church of Goffstown, New Hampshire on the 200th Anniversary of the First Settling of the Town." Goffstown, NH: Gibbs & Brown, 1941.

Potter, C.E. *The History of Manchester, Formerly Derryfield, in New-Hampshire.* Manchester, NH: C.E. Potter, 1856.

Proceedings of the Dedication of the Soldiers' Monument: Goffstown, New Hampshire, Saturday, June Seventeenth, 1916. Manchester, NH: John B. Clarke, 1916.

Shirley, Moses Gage. "The Town of Goffstown." *Granite Monthly* 24 (May 1898): 249–82.

Tolland, Vincent. "Who Was Who in the Civil War, Goffstown, NH." Goffstown, NH, 2006.

NEW HAMPSHIRE AND NEW ENGLAND

Akagi, Roy. *The Town Proprietors of the New England Colonies.* Gloucester, MA: Peter Smith, 1963.

Allen, E. John B. "The Development of New Hampshire Skiing: 1870s–1940." *Historical New Hampshire* 36 (Spring 1981): 1–37.

Bedford Historical Society. *History of Bedford, N.H., 1737–1971.* Bedford, NH: Bedford Historical Society, 1972.

Bodge, George Madison. *Soldiers in King Philip's War.* Boston: Rockwell and Churchill Press, 1896.

Chace, J., Jr. *Map of Hillsboro Co., New Hampshire from Actual Surveys.* Reprint. Boston: Smith Mason, 1858.

Cleveland, Mather. *New Hampshire Fights the Civil War.* New London, NH, 1969.

Daniell, Jere R. *Colonial New Hampshire: A History.* New York: KTO Press, 1981.

Fried, Yvonne Stahr. "'Kindling the Fires of State Patriotism': Old Home Week and the Writings of Governor Frank West Rollins." *Historical New Hampshire* 54 (Spring/Summer 1999): 3–16.

SOURCES

Gardner, William M., ed. *Towns against Tyranny: Hillsborough County New Hampshire during the American Revolution, 1775–1783.* Nashua: New Hampshire Bicentennial Commission, 1976.

Hanlan, James P. *The Working Population of Manchester, New Hampshire, 1840–1886.* Ann Arbor: University of Michigan Research Press, 1979.

Hatch, Robert McConnell. "New Hampshire at Bunker Hill." *Historical New Hampshire* 30 (Winter 1975): 215–20.

Heald, Bruce D. *Images of Rail: Boston & Maine in the 19th Century.* Portsmouth, NH: Arcadia Press, 2000.

————. *Images of Rail: Boston & Maine in the 20th Century.* Portsmouth, NH: Arcadia Press, 2001.

Herndon, Ruth Wallis. *Unwelcome Americans: Living on the Margin in Early New England.* Philadelphia: University of Pennsylvania Press, 2001.

History of Bedford, New-Hampshire, compiled on the Occasion of the One Hundredth Anniversary of the Incorporation of the Town, May 19, 1850. Boston: Alfred Mudge, 1851.

Karr, Ronald Dale. *Lost Railroads of New England.* 2nd ed. Pepperell, MA: Branch Line Press, 1996.

Lindsell, Robert M. *The Rail Lines of Northern New England.* Pepperell, MA: Branch Line Press, 2000.

Malone, Joseph J. *Pine Trees and Politics: The Naval Stores and Forest Policy in Colonial New England, 1691–1775.* Seattle: University of Washington Press, 1964.

Manning, Samuel F. *New England Masts and the King's Broad Arrow.* Kennebunk, ME: Thomas Murphy, 1979.

Morison, Elizabeth Forbes, and Elting E. Morison. *New Hampshire: A Bicentennial History.* New York: W.W. Norton, 1976.

Myers, John L. "The Beginning of Antislavery Agencies in New Hampshire, 1832–1835." *Historical New Hampshire* 25 (Fall 1970): 3–25.

————. "The Major Effect of Antislavery Agents in New Hampshire, 1835–1837." *Historical New Hampshire* 26 (Fall 1971): 3–27.

Nartonis, David K. "The 'New Divinity' Movement and Its Impact on New Hampshire's Town Churches, 1769–1849." *Historical New Hampshire* 55 (Spring 2000): 25–40.

Paradis, Wilfrid H. *Upon This Granite: Catholicism in New Hampshire, 1647–1997.* Portsmouth, NH: Peter E. Randall, 1998.

Piotrowski, Thaddeus M. *History of the American Indians in the Manchester, New Hampshire Area.* N.p., 1977.

————. *The Scots and Their Descendants in the Manchester, New Hampshire Area.* N.p., 1976.

Renda, Lex. "Credit and Culpability: New Hampshire State Politics during the Civil War." *Historical New Hampshire* 48 (Spring 1993): 3–84.

Shaffer, Duane E. *Men of Granite: New Hampshire's Soldiers in the Civil War.* Charleston: University of South Carolina Press, 2008.

Taylor, William L., ed. *Readings in New Hampshire and New England History.* New York: MSS Information Corporation, 1971.

Wallace, R. Stuart. "Carved in Granite," a lecture series offered by the New Hampshire Historical Society, Spring 2009.

Wallace, R. Stuart, and Lisa Mausolf. *New Hampshire Railroads: Historic Context Statement.* N.p., 2001.

Wallace, R. Stuart, Mike Pride, Mark Travis and Peter Wallner. "New Hampshire in the Civil War," a lecture series offered by the New Hampshire Historical Society, 2007.

ABOUT THE AUTHOR

Elizabeth Dubrulle holds a master's degree in history from the University of California at Santa Barbara, specializing in historical editing and colonial/antebellum New England. Before moving to New Hampshire in 2002, she was a senior editor for the historical reference publisher ABC-CLIO and a member of the editorial staff for the national project to edit the writings of Henry David Thoreau. She currently holds positions as an associate editor for the Colonial Society of Massachusetts, a lecturer in the Humanities Program at Saint Anselm College and a copyeditor/proofreader for the college textbook division of W.W. Norton. She also serves as chair of the Goffstown Historic District Commission/Heritage Commission and co-chair of the town's committee to plan its 250th anniversary, which will be celebrated in 2011.